KELLY BLUE

Hog Killing Time

KELLY BLUE

William Weber Johnson

FOREWORD BY TOM LEA

Texas A&M University Press

COLLEGE STATION AND LONDON

Library of Congress Cataloging in Publication Data

Johnson, William Weber, 1909–
    Kelly blue.

    Reprint of the 1960 ed. published by Doubleday, Garden
City, N. Y.
    1. Kelly, Harold Osman, 1884–1955. 2. Painters—United
States—Biography. I. Title.
[ND237.K445J6 1979]   759.13 [B]   78-21773
ISBN 0-89096-073-9

Manufactured in the United States of America

For Liz, with love

List of Illustrations

Foreword to the First Edition

HERE is an extraordinary book about an extraordinary man. I have felt certain that it would be remarkable since I first heard about it almost a decade ago, when it was little more than a dim glimmer living in the mind of my friend William Weber Johnson. He said he hoped someday to be able to write the life story of a man both of us knew and admired very much, old H. O. Kelly. Neither one of us had ever met anyone like Kelly. He was unique. Among other things, he had taught himself to paint. He had become an exceptional artist toward the end of his curiously disastrous, curiously triumphant, life.

I feel a happiness and a gratitude now that this book about Kelly is no dim glimmer but a reality I can hold in my hand, and in my heart. In my opinion, Bill Johnson has created from the material a genuine work of art that will live a long time. By it, he has broadened and deepened the meaning of the vivid life and the meaning of the good work of our friend who sleeps wrapped in the earth at Blanket, Texas.

From bales of notes, scores of letters styled in Kelly's uncommon way, old diaries, long ramblings recorded on many tapes—out of years of affectionate friendship with its subject—comes a book that is the real Kelly: funny but not too funny; sad but not too sad; hopeful but a little desperate too . . . a nineteenth-century man adrift in the twentieth; a man who repaid the world with love rather than bitterness.

Kelly's essence sprang from a more halcyon world than ours. The first sixteen years of his life were lived in the bucolic America of the nineteenth century, and a frontier frame of mind still lingered in it. It was this that shaped him. It remained, for his more than three score years and ten, his spirit's haven.

With wiry illusion, much battering, great drifting, and indestructible gusto he survived for half a century the turmoils of an alien time. The most extraordinary thing about him was that he fulfilled the life of his own spirit not by "adjusting" to a changed and changing world but by cleaving faithfully to that which had nourished and pleasured him in youth.

Ill fortunes strangely made him a fortunate man; his adversities tempered him transcendently beyond the bareness of survival. They made him an artist, a real one. And in the evening of his life he found himself able to paint its bright morning.

This book evokes not only the living presence of a man, but a good great land and overarching sky: the face of a rural America before modernity slashed it. It will remind us of an America that some of the lithographic stones of Currier & Ives recorded with charm.

But this book holds far more than the charm of some of its surfaces. A poignant dimension of reality, the sad sweet power of the truth, outreaches mere charm and reaches into us. It asks us to receive not the quaintness but the goodness in a man's mysterious struggling heart.

On these pages I find another sunlit and shadowy story of another Candide—a spry one—in worn blue denim and crimped Stetson, riding a horse when he could, plodding afoot when he had to, finding at last after all wanderings and misfortunes his garden to till. It was waiting for him. He tilled it under a blueness of sky to give us what grew there: a high gift of spirit beyond reach of all bad seasons, all inclement weathers.

Tom Lea

El Paso
January 1960

Publisher's Foreword

THE Texas A&M University Press takes pride in presenting this new and enriched edition of William Weber Johnson's unusually fine biography of H. O. "Cowboy" Kelly, a natural painter of skill and charm who left to the land he loved so well a priceless legacy of paintings which captured for all time many aspects of a fast-vanishing rural America.

Kelly Blue was first published in 1960, five years after Kelly's death, in an edition which regrettably presented none of Kelly's art except for endsheets. Despite this handicap, it received wide critical and popular acclaim. Bill Johnson knew and loved well H. O. Kelly, and his text brought vividly to life the man, his region, and his times. Unfortunately, like so many good books, *Kelly Blue* has been out of print, except in paperback, for over fifteen years.

The recent acquisition by Texas A&M University of seven of Kelly's finest paintings, together with 181 illustrated letters, makes the present edition unusually appropriate. The closeness of the relationship between Kelly and Johnson is attested to by the fact that most of the letters in the A&M collection are addressed to Johnson. Like Charles M. Russell, Kelly enlivened nearly all his letters with completely delightful free-hand color sketches. (The seven paintings mentioned above now hang permanently in the collection of the Memorial Student Center of Texas A&M University; the letters are in the University's archives.)

The Press is grateful to Mr. and Mrs. William Weber Johnson, Mrs. Daniel Longwell, Mr. William Cooper, Mrs. Agnes Davis, Mr. Charles Stewart, Mr. Thomas C. Yantis, Miss Mabel Eubank, Mr. Stanley Marcus, Mr. Richard Bywaters, Mr. W. Lee Watson, and the Dallas Museum of Fine Arts, who made paintings available for this book.

We are likewise grateful to Tom Lea, the Southwest's remarkably talented author and artist, for permission to reprint the foreword he wrote for the 1960 edition. This foreword is so exactly right for the book that we have resisted the temptation to ask Tom Lea to expand it for the new edition.

Finally, we express heartfelt thanks to J. Harold Dunn of Amarillo for his generous gift which made possible the enrichment of the present edition with so many fine color plates.

KELLY BLUE

"I hope you live to be very old and supple and learn to drink beer at 7 A.M. And when you write a book I will come and regale you with tales that will make folks sit up and read all night. And all true! And all with a moral. Adventures of a hired man with a loose foot and a roving eye, as told to Wm. Weber Johnson. Vocals and appropriate illustrations by yours truly. A book for open and mature minds. . . ."

H. O. K. 8–9–51

Chapter 1

IN the calm and quiet of the predawn darkness the old man stretched himself in the bed and, turning, glanced at the east window. The faintest tinge of gray told his practiced eye that it would, in a few minutes, be 4:30 A.M. He reached a thick-knuckled, heavily veined hand to the battery-operated radio on a chair beside the bed and turned a knob. There was a click and a light illuminated the dial, already set for a station in Omaha. Music filtered thinly into the room. Polka music, bouncy, brassy, with a strong drumbeat. "The Green Willow Polka." "The Sev Polka." Then a waltz. Then Kuckler's *Laendler*, and in the dark the old man smiled to himself, tapped a big toe against the iron footrail of the bed and dreamily waved a hand back and forth to the music. With closed eyes he saw happy couples dancing on the green grass. The music ended, and he thought of other people who might have been listening. Ranchers in the sand hills along the North Platte, corn farmers in Kansas, wheat growers on the dusty plains, truckers drumming across west Texas with loads of cattle for the Fort Worth yards, German-speaking farmers in the Texas hill country preparing to go out into their tidy meadows and well-kept fields and orchards. The music began again, and his mind was once more with the dancers, happy, plump, and pleasing to the eye, whirling gracefully to the sweet, lively tune; the men red-faced and well scrubbed in clean work clothes; the women round-cheeked and buxom in bright-colored dresses. They drew beer from kegs, poured cider from pitchers, and ate heartily from tables heaped with food—whole chickens and turkeys and hams, wheels of cheese, coils of sausage, tubs of potato salad, bowls of jams and jellies, jars of honey and great platters of apples, grapes, peaches. They ate and drank and danced again in the lovely world of the old man's mind.

The half-hour program ended. He switched off the radio, swung his feet to the floor and stood up. His arms and legs were corded with hard, thin muscles and thick veins.

His shoulders were stooped, somewhat crooked but still heavy with power. His belly was flat and his legs were bowed. He shrugged into a faded blue work shirt, stepped into a stiff pair of levis, thrust his feet into comfortable house shoes. He walked through a door to the back gallery and poured water from a bucket into a tin basin. Then he sloshed water on his stiff gray-black hair and scrubbed his face, kneading the close-set quizzical eyes. He faced a broken piece of mirror nailed to the wall and ran a pocket comb through the brush of hair with little result. He then took a gray-white felt hat from a nail on the wall, punched out the crown so that it was without crease or indentation. Still looking in the mirror shard, he placed it squarely on his head, then punched the crown and tugged at the brim until it suited him.

Stubby, the little tawny dog, was running in circles of joy in the yard. Booger, the bobtailed cat, rubbed against the old man's legs and purred gratingly. The old man stooped to pet him, running a hand over the ear that had been permanently crimped in a fight with a boar coon and thought: Like me, his looks are against him and, like me, he doesn't care.

Soft morning light sifted through the old mulberry tree and warmed the magenta-stained earth beneath it. Under the fresh lacy leaves of the mesquite tree the light was clear and green as the bottom of a spring. Somewhere a mockingbird whistled his last song of the night; a rain crow moaned, and on all sides roosters called.

He walked around the house to a roughly built shed, sitting at a crazy angle on its underpinnings. For the hundredth or the thousandth time as he looked at it he remembered the angle at which he had once worn a derby hat, many years ago, when he and three friends drank and sang together, he singing bass and drinking heavy ale while the others stayed on beer. The more ale he drank and the more songs he sang, the lower the derby slipped over his right eye.

From inside the shed came the nicker of the mare. He lowered the bars, slipped a halter on the mare and led her first to the water trough and then through the wire gate to the little pasture where the Johnson grass was still fresh and green from the summer rains. The mare lowered her head and began to graze but stood still while the old man ran his hands admiringly down her sides and flanks. The dull sorrel of the coarse winter coat was gone now, and the mare was a smooth chestnut with gold highlights in the rising sun.

The old man returned to the house, made coffee and took a cup to the front porch. He sat on the step, smoked a hand-rolled cigarette and listened for the morning sounds he knew so well: the rough cry of turkey cocks, squealing pigs, bleating lambs, the bugling of a stallion and the muttering of a bull. And the morning cry of the jackass, a sound which most people found hideous and disturbing but which he loved.

They had all been real once, a long time ago. Now only a few hens clucked in the yard, and in the little pasture the mare pulled and chewed on the Johnson grass.

He finished his cigarette and returned to the room where he had slept. He gave a quick yank to the bedclothes to straighten them. Then he sat himself on a high bench at a table by the window. From a cardboard shoebox he took tubes of oil paint and began mixing them, using an old water color slanted tray instead of a palette. He stared at the mixture through a pair of steel-rimmed spectacles that rode low on the battered nose which he said had reached its present shape and coloration only with much effort and expense. He paused to roll and light another cigarette. Then he placed a clean white gesso board flat on the table before him and began painting the top half of it—a solid blue. In an hour he had finished three boards, each covered from top to middle with the same blue. The blue was a little bluer than the sky, a little brighter; clear and light, unchanging and unfailing.

He set the boards aside to dry and returned to the porch. Seated in a rocker, he looked out across the caliche road, the field beyond the road and the stream, bordered by willows and sumac, beyond the field. Long ago Indian women had come there to wash their blankets, rubbing them on stones in the creek bed and spreading them on the sunny banks to dry, squares of color in the sun, with the brown-shining, naked children playing in the water. He wished that he could have seen it, and he went on to think of things he had seen and loved.

His grandfather's house in Ohio, red brick with white trim and four stately chimneys. The elms and the apple trees, the red barn with the cider mill, and farm wagons drawn up loaded with apples for the mill, Rambos, Jonathans, Astrachans, and small boys filching apples from the wagons.

A red-eared white bull standing in the blackened door of a charcoal kiln in upper Michigan while a boy on horseback tries to coax him out.

Cowboys riding through a street, their horses' hoofs raising puffs of dust, the conchos on their saddles glinting, their kerchiefs bright in the sun and wind, and women and girls waving from doors and windows.

The low green sand hills of Nebraska in the spring with the sedge and cactus blooming, and, later, yellow stacks of prairie hay, shimmering in the summer heat.

A giant Negro driving five yoke of oxen in the Arkansas swamps, hauling thick white oak logs, the driver's boots splashing in the water, his whip snaking out and exploding over the backs of the cattle without touching them. The oxen of all colors. Red, black, white, brindle, dun.

A revival meeting in a brush arbor, the preacher's arms waving, his eyes rolling. And beyond, farm women setting up tables and unpacking baskets for dinner on the grounds.

An Osage family in their rubber-tired surrey.

Two quarter horses finishing a sprint.

A Mexican herdsman driving goats.

A family planting a spring garden.

Farmers killing and dressing hogs, hanging the carcasses, giving the bladders to children for playthings, steam rising from the caldrons and a thin skiff of snow on the ground, deeper on the faraway hills.

A cable ferry crossing a fast-flowing little river carrying a wagon and a span of mules and an old lady sitting in the wagon, her parasol raised against the sun.

He often said he had a million pictures in his head. Or ten million. Talking with friends and neighbors he sometimes would, for no clear reason, begin describing scenes from long ago, the way people lived and worked together and took their pleasures. These were the pictures that he painted, drawn from his mind, clean and sharp, some of them true memories, more of them the way he wished the memories to be. Working as painfully and slowly as he did, he could never finish, could never do all of them. And this was his only grave complaint about the way a man's life runs its course. And he felt sorry for young people who had not seen the things that he had seen. He had lived in an interesting time.

He changed from house shoes to boots, brought the mare from the pasture, saddled her and rode down the caliche road toward the little town of Blanket, Texas. Painting could wait until evening when he had had a full day to think and remember.

Chapter 2

HIS name was Harold Osman Kelly. He preferred to be called H. O. Kelly or H. O. or simply Kelly. But people had taken to calling him Grandpa Kelly and Old Man Kelly and Cowboy Kelly, none of which he cared for.

He was a grandfather, all right, and proud of his grandsons. But he saw no reason for others to call him Grandpa.

As for Old Man Kelly, he really didn't consider himself old. He had been through enough years and hard times to break many men. But he still had some vigor and much yearning and at least a little vanity. All his people, the Kellys and the Osmans, were long-lived. His great-great-grandmother had been born before the Revolution and had lived to one hundred and four. Kelly saw no reason why he should not better her. His life might not be much more than half over, he liked to think. There were so many things he had to do, so many roads to ride. He still wanted a little farm of his own in the hill country, and he would still like to see Spain. Spain first, and then England and Ireland. It would take many years, but he was able. Only the other day he had ridden Babe, the mare, into Blanket for tobacco and mail and a visit with Ernest Allen at the drugstore. When he left the drugstore an old, old man was sitting there in the sunshine and watched him swing himself into the saddle. "You get on a horse just like a kid, Kelly," the old man said. "How old are you, anyway?" And Kelly replied, "Sixty-six, but then I'm half horse," and this had pleased both of them.

Cowboy Kelly? It had been a long time since he had worked as a cowhand, a long time since he had ridden through blizzards in Wyoming to collect backdrifted cattle, a longer time since he had gone with the wild bunch in Arizona on Saturday nights, riding through the tules, as the fellows said—the back way into town. People might just as well call him Farmer Kelly, he thought, or Stockman Kelly or Cotton

Picker Kelly (although of all work he liked this the least). Or if they had to name a man for his job, they might call him Bullwhacker Kelly, for there were few men still alive who had, as he had, driven oxen in the swamps and thickets of Arkansas, and he was very proud of this distinction.

Best of all, he would have liked to be known as Kelly the Stud Horse and Jack Man. All his life he had loved horses and donkeys and mules, had lived and worked with them, bred and cared for them. He had driven them to a plow and had driven them eight-up on a freight wagon, the leather ribbons laced between his knowing fingers. He had raced them on the snow path in Ohio on Sunday afternoons long ago and he had ridden them in quarter-mile sprints in Texas, his hat jammed down on his ears and an unused willow switch in his teeth. He had ridden broncs in country rodeos in Wyoming and Nebraska, and he had harnessed and worked horses that others said could not be handled. He had a gentling hand and voice and he still broke colts for his friends and helped when they bred their mares. He understood the strange mind of the donkey and his family, and although he didn't care much for folklore he liked the Mexican belief that the dark, furry cross on the donkey's withers was a badge for having carried the Virgin Mary and the baby Jesus. He loved stallions and had no fear of them, taking pleasure in their noise and excitement. He did not like either geldings or men who castrated horses. He preferred his horses entire, no less than men. And if he now owned and rode a mare instead of a stallion, it was not a concession to age and infirmity but only because stallions made his wife nervous.

But people like characters and like for their characters to have nicknames. Kelly knew this and it was all right. It was kindly meant. His paintings had made him a character, and people could call him whatever they liked. The paintings were selling. Not for much, when he considered how many weeks and months it usually took him to paint a picture. Still, it was money, and he was not, he often said, like those Wyoming cows that can make it on wind and scenery. This was the first money he had had, really, since '29 on the High Plains when wheat was bountiful and profitable, when everyone had money. Even Kelly. Before the dirt storms got so bad.

Kelly had made pictures all his life, with ink or pencil or crayons or water color, and just recently with oils. He seldom had money at Christmas or for birthdays or weddings, and he had long ago begun making little pictures of things and places he had seen to send to relatives and friends as remembrances. At first, anyway, the pictures were of things he saw. Then, more and more, pictures of things he remembered or thought he remembered.

Recently friends had arranged an exhibition of his paintings at Dallas, and great crowds of people had come to see his work. There had been write-ups in newspapers and magazines and orders came in for his paintings, many from far away.

And people came to see him, which he liked. Any man who had lived on the plains and seen his neighbors leave, one by one, beaten by the dust, leaving the land dark and empty and lonely—any man who had lived through this loved company and visiting.

Some came as curiosity seekers, just as they would go to see a two-headed calf or a gallows where a man had died. Some came because they had a large, generic enthusiasm for Art, and they had heard this old man described by knowing critics as a home-grown Brueghel, another George Caleb Bingham, another Eastman Johnson.

And others came because they liked what they heard and saw of the paintings, loving and understanding the things with which Kelly dealt and the way he did it. It was a rural America that had largely disappeared a half-century before. The paintings were filled with lively, well-drawn little figures going about their business and their pleasure, riding and driving horses, handling stock, drinking beer, going to church, plowing fields, dancing waltzes and polkas, bedding down in a wagon yard, making sirup, flirting or betting on a horse race. Everyone was well fed and happy. Old people were dignified and respected. Women were courted with grace and courtesy. Men dealt with each other on equal terms, and small white and Negro boys swam together in the streams in naked freedom.

All, the curiosity seekers as well as the serious ones, were made welcome at the frail little house that had been scoured by the abrasive Texas wind until it was as bare of paint as the old man's face was lacking in guile. They would be shown the small, dark room where Kelly worked, bending over a makeshift table. They would be shown the work in progress, the white canvasses with only the unchanging blue sky painted in, the sure line of the horizon, the ghosts of buildings to be, and the many small figures, sketched first in innocent nakedness so that Kelly could get their proportions and the movement of their arms and legs right before giving them clothes. He would tell of his enemies: the ashes and flakes of Bull Durham that fell from his cigarette as he leaned, working, over the table. The gnats that came through the partially screened windows at night, attracted by his working lamp, to become stuck in the wet paint. And the dust that sometimes still came to plague him, the dust he had fought in the Plains for so many years, still seeking him out when there was a strong northwest blow. Then he would have to stop and shut the unfinished paintings in a trunk until the dust would settle or blow away.

Whatever painting he was working on had live antecedents for the characters. They were all people Kelly had known or seen. This was old Granny Kaufman, coming to town on her mare, Lyddy, carrying her basket of eggs to sell. And this was old Gid Tierney who had fought at Shiloh and who, when he was drinking corn, would ride his horse into town at a full run, long white mustaches flying, giving the rebel yell. This man pondering a horse trade was his friend Ed Nabors. This was old Dick Teague.

All the visitors were treated well. Kelly would bring cool cans of beer from the stone-lined storm cellar and play polkas on the old hand-wound phonograph that had been inherited from his beloved brother, Quill. The old machine scratched and rumbled, but it made no difference with a lively tune, and Kelly would dance a few steps, his stiff boots raising puffs of dust from the old boards of the porch. He would take them to the pasture to admire Babe, show them the old Miles City saddle and tell how Stubby, the feist dog, had once caught and killed a hawk. He would tell of the thirty states in which he had lived, worked and traveled, of the many kinds of work he had done and the kinds of people he had known. He would tell tales, salty or moral or both, sometimes gauged to fit his visitors, sometimes not. He might describe favorite scenes from Dickens and Stevenson, quote Chaucer or Bernal Diaz with relish, and tell how Magner, the horse and stock man, agreed with Marcus Terentius Varro on the best conditions for breeding horses. In describing scenes that he hoped to paint he might recite one of the many Psalms that he loved or a favorite old hymn, not as a demonstration of his piety but rather that he and the men who had sung the Psalms and written the hymns had seen and understood many things together.

He was a man of wit and wisdom and, in most things, humility. And perhaps he was a man of greatness. Yet he lived in a state of near poverty. He neither apologized for it nor boasted of his poverty. There was no virtue in it, no rejection of or withdrawal from the material world. He liked creature comforts. He had had some bad years, that was all, and he would laugh, "About fifty of them." Still, one day he would get a little ahead and would buy a farm in the hill country. Sixty acres, with forty in good pasture, and twenty in level black bottom land along one of the lovely little spring-fed creeks. The twenty acres would be divided into five four-acre plots, planted to feed crops and carefully rotated. He would have a good stud horse for riding and pleasure and the money that could be made from stud fees, and a pair of fat jennies to pull the plow and bray for him at sunup and dusk. There would be a tavern not too far away, for beer and laughter and dancing and good talk on Saturday nights; a church for Sunday mornings, and a little race course where a man with an able horse and a willing spirit could find some competition on a Sunday afternoon.

Often Kelly would sense an unspoken question in the mind of his visitor. If the visitor seemed sympathetic and worthy and not just inquisitive, Kelly would tell something of his beginnings and his people.

Chapter 3

"THERE'S mighty fine people behind me and they were always good and kind to me though I was a scapegrace. I have consorted with a rather rough bunch and oftentimes my foot has slipped. I have some Irish ancestry, devious but powerful, along with a love of improvident ways, black-headed blue-eyed women and strong waters. I have always liked a few on a Saturday night, some lively songs—none of your mournful songs for me—slow waltzes with tender-eyed ladies and fast horses dusting out on a Sunday afternoon. High spirits and pleasure and no one hurt.

"My father's people came from St. Galen, Switzerland, where they had been led from Ireland hundreds of years before. My father was one of nine and his people were blacksmiths, mechanics and Presbyterians. Most of them lived in Pennsylvania and worked for the Pennsylvania Railroad, although I had one uncle who was a tailor in the summertime and in the winter he would take his knives and steels and become the community butcher, riding a fine grey horse that lived to a venerable age. And another uncle married a Catholic woman, and their daughters were the loveliest of my many cousins.

"My mother's people were German on both sides, and I was born at 8 P.M. on March 6, 1884, in my grandfather Osman's house in Bucyrus, Ohio, a beautiful county seat town with brick-paved streets and elms and maples bending over the streets. My grandfather's house was large, built of red brick, and is still standing. My grandfather Osman had eight fireplaces and three Seth Thomas clocks and everything was very nice. The walk to the privy was paved with brick and sheltered by a grape arbor, purple concords and red catawbas, and you could gather a hatful as you walked along. Inside the privy was papered with old circus posters, and I remember always being scared damn near to death by the blood-sweating hippopotamus, not knowing at the time that they were herbivorous. My grandfather had a soft gray beard and kindly brown eyes and he came from Mannheim, Germany. As a young man he had often danced all night in Germany and France. In Bucyrus he made wagons to take people to the West, and he manufactured brick and tile to pave the streets and drain the good blackland farms. A noble monument, I think. And he had a steam cider mill. When my brother Quill, short for Walter Aquilla, and I visited there as boys we could count as many as thirty wagons loaded with apples waiting for the mill. We would sample each wagon and would often get the green-apple quickstep which my grandfather would cure with Jamaica ginger and brandy.

"Have you ever tasted cider made from Rambo apples and properly racked off? One of the sorriest sonsabitches I ever worked for was a retired schoolteacher who wore side whiskers and said long family prayers and wouldn't swear but just beat the hell out of his horses when he got mad. But I'll say this for him. He could make the best cider. He would let the frost hit his Rambos and then gather them and take them to the mill. That cider had a bouquet that was lovely and salubrious.

"My grandfather learned to make and care for and love cider in the old country, and he always had twelve or fifteen barrels in his brick cellar, from the sweet champagne variety to old stone fence that would knock your head off. He would tap the barrels with a little whip-handled mallet, and it was fine drinking from one apple crop to the next. His cider pitcher was never empty, nor the plate of gingerbread beside it.

"When I was four my father took us to Missouri Valley, Iowa, where he worked as a blacksmith for the Fremont, Elkhorn and Missouri Valley Railroad. It was a feeding point on the road and the cattle cars stopped there. Big longhorn steers from Texas that had been driven across the Plains to fatten in Montana and Nebraska and then be shipped to Chicago, their horns so wide they would break in the car doors. Indians would come to town and trade in baskets and herb medicines and spotted ponies. On summer nights we slept outdoors and thought we could hear the corn growing. And on Sunday afternoons Father, after being on his feet in the shop all week, would take us boys for walks along the Missouri River bluffs to see where the cliff swallows lived.

"My father always liked a high place, for the view, and so do I. The best way to do it is on a horse. South of San Saba, before you get to old Cherokee, there's a line of hills with grass all the way to the top. The skyline is grass, with little live-oak mottes sticking up against the sky. Later on it will be Naples yellow, but just now it would be gray-green with little patches of pink where the needle grass is. The only way to really see it is on a horse. Ride for the ridge and see what's on the other side. You can be riding through pastures like that and you'll smell something very fragrant, just like when you walk through mignonette. It's wild grape blossoms, you know, hanging on a tree. If you're driving in a car, you don't get that. But on a horse the horse knows where you're going and you don't have to bother with him. You smell things and you see things. And you've got to do that if you're going to get any subjects to paint. If you don't go around and see things, why, then, after a while you're just trotting around in the damn muck.

"Then we moved to Marquette in the upper peninsula of Michigan. It is a dour country, and I remember being frightened by many things. The fog whistle from Lighthouse Point. The ruins of a house where a widow woman had burned to death, the charred studs black in the snow. Quill and I slept in an upstairs room where the cold was the still kind that gets into your bones. We often neglected our prayers, it was so cold, and then we would lie in bed and worry because we had. From our window we could see Lake Superior. Each year one of the fishing boats would try to make one more trip before the ice closed in and would go aground on Whitefish Point or get wrecked and the bodies would not come up until summer, swollen up and the faces nibbled away by fish. Jimmy Smith, the only colored boy in our neighborhood, taught me to fight. He had to fight because he was colored, and I had to fight because I was small. He died of what they called galloping consumption. The men from the logging camps would come in town and fight in the streets when they were paid off in the spring. Spring sometimes didn't come until June, and often there would be arbutus in the snow in May.

"But there were many nice things, too. In the fall of the year they would bring in carloads of horses to go to the logging camps for the winter. Big fine draft horses. My brother and I would risk a whipping to go to the barns and walk in the stalls and pet each one. Never got bitten or kicked, which is a source of pride with me. They plowed the sidewalks with four-horse teams in the winter, but they let the snow pack the streets and every vehicle went on runners. All the horses had bells, many of them sweet-sounding Swiss bells. There were some wealthy families and they had wonderful turnouts, both single and double teams, mostly of the trotting type and, happy to say, none of the docked tails and gag reins they use to torment horses in Eastern cities. Beautiful horses, smallish dainty-stepping horses. The double-seated sleighs would have plumes on the swan-shaped dashboard, and the flowing scarves of the ladies and the bells jingling, it was all very nice.

"Sometimes they would drive herds of cows through the streets, and the first picture I remember drawing was of one of these herds. I included a bull mounting a cow and I got a whipping from my mother.

"Summers we used to go to Julius Gogarn's farm near Munising Bay, and it was wonderful. Old Julius was a Civil War soldier who had first had a trading post for the Indians and then this farm. Snug log buildings, chinked with white plaster and whitewashed, inside and out, and a bathtub hewn and burned from a big log. Chippewa Indians would come to dig the potato crop, and they would bring us venison to eat. The cattle were on open range on the cutover timber land where the timothy and the red clover grew well. One of my chores and pleasures was to bring in the cattle in the evening. I rode a little gray mare named Bird, safe and secure from all alarms save the deer flies which made us both miserable. I would generally find the cows near the old charcoal kilns where they went to get away from the deer flies.

"I never really liked school and at first I would run away from it. Just go home. But I had some good and pleasant teachers, and I'm grateful that they taught me to read because reading has given me great pleasure all my life. There was a good library and I always took out books. Prescott's books on the conquest of Mexico and Peru. Two volumes each. Those old historians could really write to make you see things. And that's where I discovered Dickens. I think *Pickwick Papers* is my favorite book. I've read it many times, and when friends have been sick or blue I've read it to them to pick them up.

"I finished two years of high school in Marquette and then we moved to Scott-dale, Pennsylvania, where my father was to work in the shops, and I decided I'd go to school no more. I can remember hearing my father and mother talk at night, saying that I should go to school, but if I would not I must go to work. And that the shops would take on no apprentices until fall. The next day I got my first full-time job. I was just turned sixteen, a half-century ago, and I know how I disappointed my folks. How I come to do it I can't explain, because all my people were solid and permanent, sort of, thrifty and good. I did have a cousin in Altoona who took to rambling, leaving home at fourteen. Went to England with a load of army mules and at seventeen was running a steam shovel in Culebra Cut. He was a couple of years older than I was, a fine barroom scrapper and quite a hero in my eyes. But our people seldom mentioned him.

"It was the spring of the year and I'd been prowling the farming country thereabouts, in western Pennsylvania, looking at the rich farms and admiring the stock. The Mennonite farmers, with square black beards and black hats and thrifty ways, were kind and polite to a boy who was interested in their farms and animals.

"I asked one of them if he could use a hand and he said that he could not, but that a neighbor named Arthur Porter, just over the hill, could. I walked over the hill to Porter's and just started in helping. Porter was Scotch-Irish, a big kindly man with chin whiskers but a clean-shaven upper lip. He had big fine plowing horses, plowing with a jerkline, so instead of pulling line to guide them you would just tell them 'gee' or 'haw.' That's the way they work the big freight teams in the West, you know.

"Well, I asked him if he wanted to hire a hand and he said yes, he could use one, and he gave me the plow. I told him I had never plowed any, but I wanted to be a farmer. He just smiled and gave me the plow and told me to go ahead. I never had anything in my life jerk the hell out of me like that plow did. It was set to plow perfectly and all you had to do was keep it on course. I was trying to hold it, you know, instead of letting it run itself, and it just jerked and whipped me around. I was so beat up at noon I just wanted to cry, thinking I wasn't man enough to plow. I was sixteen but I was small for my age.

"So Porter came out then, from his dinner, and he showed me how to do it, with just a light touch. That helped me and we plowed a good long full day. Plowing is very nice when you do it right. You can always see what you have done and what you've got to do.

"We were eating supper, just about dusk, out on the back porch, and here came my father and my brother, Quill, looking for me. When my dad talked to Porter I think he was kind of proud. Porter told him what I had said, that I hadn't farmed any but I wanted to be a farmer and I was trying very hard. My father laughed and said, 'Well, we'll just leave him here until fall.'

"I was there all through corn planting and into the harvest. Porter paid me eight dollars a month and my board, and it was wonderful board. I slept there at his house, a big old Pennsylvania farmhouse made for two families, the old man's and the son's. I stayed there just like I belonged to him, and I saved my money. I was saving to buy a colt. I could buy a good weanling colt for twenty-five dollars, and on days that were too wet to work in the fields Porter took me with him to the horse and cattle sales. Also I bought a book, *Magner's Horse and Stock Book*. I still have it and treasure it. It is still the best authority on veterinary subjects. It even goes into beekeeping and there is a fine chapter on training horses. Magner had been a traveling showman, could drive horses without lines, things like that.

"Porter had two unmarried daughters, and they were nice to me, too. They liked to go to parties and I would drive for them. They didn't believe in dancing, but they played all kinds of party games, name games and kissing games and Jolly Miller. That was a song game where they kind of danced, singing:

> Here's to the miller boy that works in the mill,
> He works all day by running of the rill.
> One hand in the hopper, the other in the sack
> The ladies turn bowed and the gents turn back.

They all wheeled and danced to that but they didn't call it dancing.

"I worked there until late summer when I had a sunstroke. Then I went home and got a job as an apprentice machinist in the shops. My folks would have given me an education, but I was bound to work, and my father helped me the only way he could, getting me a job in the place where he worked. Wasn't that nice? It was really a fine opportunity. The year was 1900, the beginning of the twentieth century, and if I could have stuck to it I might have been as successful and respected a man as my father was."

Chapter 4

KELLY never really felt at ease with the twentieth century; most of the things he liked belonged to the nineteenth. Of all the material, mechanical and electronic wonders that the new century brought, he looked with favor, in late years, only on the radio. Not that he understood or was even interested in its workings; they baffled him. But his old battery-driven radio set was, in the last years of his life, never far away from his bedside or work table, ready to bring him, at the flick of a switch, his beloved polkas, waltzes and *Laendlers*.

As for all the rest of the marvels of the century, he just didn't care. Television, on the few occasions that he watched it, bored him. He saw his last motion picture in 1929 in Dalhart, Texas, and passed the remaining quarter-century of his life without any desire to see another one.

He had never, in a house of his own, lived with electricity or a furnace or running water. It was a matter of economics rather than eccentricity or deliberate non-conformity. But his only vocal complaint was that his heating system—a fireplace on cool summer evenings and an iron stove in the winter—frequently overheated his head and left his feet cold. For the rest of the conveniences of a mechanical age, he seemed to miss them no more than he missed never having owned a frock coat or a silk hat. He would not, if he could help it, ride on an air-conditioned railway car or bus. He never rode in an airplane, worried about friends who did and sturdily refused to ship his paintings by air.

Communication with his fellow men had always been important for him. He was an artful and ready conversationalist. He was a loyal, tireless writer of letters to family and friends. He seldom sold a painting without becoming a regular correspondent of the purchaser. But he never took kindly to the telephone. He would, with a telephone in his hand, suddenly become tongue-tied, and, holding the instrument at arm's length, barely whisper toward it.

His idea of warming a chilled engine on a cold morning was to drench it in gasoline and set a match to it, which sometimes had spectacular results. The fairly rudimentary mechanics of a windmill puzzled him. When he took his own mill apart to fix the rods or replace the leathers, he usually called on his neighbors to help him reassemble it. He was alarmed by the coaster brakes on his grandsons' bicycles and was certain they would cause accidents. He maintained that the only way to plow a garden plot was with a donkey, and that nothing good could come of tractors. Power garden plows, which some of his neighbors were beginning to use, were, he was convinced, deadly. "Don't use them," he would advise, "and never let anyone leave one around where you can tinker with it if you want to live to be a good *old* man. They will kill you off. They go like hell, poppity-pop and hellity-scoot. They suck themselves right down into the ground and won't ease up at the word as a good jack or jenny will."

In the High Plains where everyone used tractors to farm their wide fields Kelly had kept right on plowing, listing and cultivating with teams of horses. A gasoline- or kerosene-driven machine was alien to farming as he understood it and liked to think of it. One spring when his plowing had been almost hopelessly delayed by the weather Kelly accepted the offer of help from a tractor-owning neighbor, Newt Holt. Holt was tired, having just finished his own plowing.

Kelly eyed the tractor and gang plow belligerently and said, "Newt, you just lie down and rest. I'll run this thing." Anyone, he thought, who could handle horses could manage this.

Kelly climbed in the seat and started off, opening the throttle wide. The tractor roared and rattled and took off across the field, the gang plow veering wildly, first one way, then another. They reached the end of the field, and Kelly apparently was unable to slow the machine for the turn. Tractor and plow roared through the fence, jolted across borrow ditch and road, broke through another fence. Kelly, hanging on desperately, finally swung the machine in a wide circle, crashed through the fences again and was well back into his own field before he wrestled the tractor to a halt, wheels and gang plow trailing barbed wire and fence posts like a mass of seaweed.

"Why didn't you tell me you couldn't run her?" Holt shouted.

"Tractors!" Kelly snorted, as though the word were obscene, and went to the corral to hitch up his team.

Grover Dabney ran the gasoline station in Blanket, and at Dabney's station farmers, ranchers, truckers and other citizens, Kelly among them, gathered to gossip, loaf and trade jokes. Kelly enjoyed the time he spent there, and he liked Grover Dabney. But he often told him that a station could never compare with the old-fashioned livery barn as a social center. Gasoline and oil might not smell bad, but they didn't smell good the way hay, manure and horseflesh did. The jokes picked up by truckers on their rounds somehow weren't as funny as those told by drummers when they came to the stables to hire a rig. And cars and trucks did not inspire the kind of easy unhurried companionship that horse-riding, horse-working, horse-loving men enjoyed.

During the last twenty-five years of his life Kelly owned a succession of automobiles, but never a new one. The right price for a car, he thought, was about fifty dollars—certainly no more than a hundred. If a man had more than that to spend he should get a horse; a man was healthier, happier and far safer on a horse.

In the High Plains he had first owned an old Model T Ford, and in his memory it was the only good automobile ever built. When, finally, the first car would no longer run, he traded it for an almost equally decrepit Model A Ford with a gear-shift instead of the simple old-fashioned transmission. The changeover crossed Kelly's threshold of mechanical understanding. At first he could not stop the car. On one of his first runs he drove it to a neighbor's, circled the house twice while shouting some message and took off down the dusty road. He did not trust himself to drive it in traffic, and on Saturdays, when the Kellys went to Dalhart to do their shopping, Kelly would leave the car at the railroad overpass and walk into town. He would struggle back to the car, loaded with packages of groceries and sacks of feed, and when his friends chided him about the heavy load he was carrying he would say that this was nothing. Why, once back in Arkansas when he was moving from one rent farm to another he walked six miles carrying a sow and a litter of pigs and dragging a harrow.

His driving speed was never high but it was unvaried, making no allowance for the rutted, dusty or muddy roads. Springs broke and tires blew out but they brought no change in his driving habits. He would make his wife and daughter ride in the rear seat, giving him plenty of arm and leg room to manage the car. Eggs and cream being taken to town spilled, broke and spattered. Groceries and feed brought back from town often burst their sacks under the pounding. Coal and other heavy supplies which he sometimes hauled in a little trailer behind the car frequently broke loose,

Ohio Farm Scene

The Street

unnoticed, and ended up in a ditch, where Kelly would find them, hours later, by lantern light.

Although he came, in time, to be a little more at ease in an automobile, each car that he owned was a succession of disasters, all of which deepened his misgivings. Rods and bearings burned, wires shorted, metal rusted and batteries died. When the state of Texas ordered that all automobiles must be inspected for conformity to certain minimum safety standards Kelly was rebellious. He resented, instinctively, any governmental invasion of what he regarded as solely his own business; he also knew that his car would never pass muster. He got out his paint box, carefully painted a counterfeit "approved" sticker and pasted it on his windshield.

Even without the mechanical failures there was no sympathy between Kelly and automobiles. Under his control an automobile was unresponsive. The hands and mind and voice that could calm wild horses and guide trained ones with grace and precision were singularly ineffective in charge of a car. Getting a car started was always a problem. But, having done so, Kelly would often allow the motor to run while he had another cup of coffee, just as he had so often saddled and ridden cold-back horses for a while before breakfast to get the pitching and bucking out of their systems before starting the day's work. But, instead of improving during this period of grace, the automobile would frequently overheat and stop.

He would have front brakes detached so that on quick stops the rear of the car would settle down as a horse does when suddenly reined. He achieved the effect, but only at the expense of stopping power. A sudden application of the brakes would send the car skidding, Kelly said, "sidewise, like a boar hog going to war."

He turned corners squarely, as he might on a sure-footed, quick-pivoting horse. And he distracted companions by sitting sideways in the driver's seat, just as he might in a saddle, gesturing and pointing and seldom looking at the road, letting the car find its own way, just as a good horse would.

For Kelly the automobile had, in his last years, one virtue. It was useful for beer runs. Not that he drank so much beer; a single can or bottle might last him for hours. But he liked to have beer on hand, and, living in a dry county, it was necessary to make occasional trips to nearby counties to keep up his supply. For this a car was all right. But you couldn't drive a car up on Salt Mountain after a rain to see the live oaks olive green against the fresh-washed limestone cliffs and the goats shining like silver.

A car should have been handy for trips to the beautiful hill country of Texas, which he loved, but after running off the road several times while admiring the scenery he wisely resolved to use a bus instead.

An accident was inevitable and in an urban area it would have come much sooner. One day while driving across the state highway near his home, admiring the fields on either side, Kelly drove directly into the path of a speeding car. The other driver tried valiantly to avoid a crash but it was impossible, and Kelly was sideswiped and his car demolished. When he regained consciousness in the Brownwood Hospital he expressed thankfulness that no one else was hurt and, secondly, that now he would not have to paint his car, a project for which he had been saving odd remnants of paint.

Friends, hoping to save him from more trouble, carefully scraped the counterfeit inspection sticker from the shattered windshield. Having been involved in an accident and, miraculously, having survived, Kelly was fined ten dollars and required to take a driver's examination. When he had first got a license it was necessary only to demonstrate that he could start, steer and stop. Kelly was seldom testy, but the new examination brought out what testiness he had. The examining officer was young, brusque and totally disinterested in Kelly's views on horsemanship. And his dismissal was quite abrupt when Kelly turned one of his square corners, knocking over and breaking two test parking poles.

"People," he would say, "are the way God made them. Some like engines and some like horses. If I had taken more kindly to mechanical things, my life might have been different but I'm not sure that I would have liked it. I might have become a successful machinist as most of my people were. But I didn't, and in a way that started me to roaming.

"When I went to work as an apprentice machinist in the shops at Scottdale, a boy of sixteen, my uncle Ike was master mechanic and my father master blacksmith. Dad didn't want me to learn the blacksmith's trade. It was too hard and you couldn't go high enough, although he went as high as you could.

"The shops belonged to the H. C. Frick Coal and Coke Company, part of the Carnegie steel outfit, and we worked on those little mining locomotives, the engines that fuel the coke ovens, and on the steam pumps for the mines. I had a wonderful opportunity to learn and my folks had hopes for me. I got seventy-five cents a day, seven and one-half cents an hour for the first year, and I gave half of it to my mother.

The second year I got ten cents an hour, a dollar a day. A good farmhand, like I wanted to be, only got twelve or fifteen dollars a month, but then he got his board, too. If I'd stayed to become a journeyman machinist, I would have got twenty-two and one-half cents an hour, and that was good money. And a journeyman machinist could go anywhere in the world to work, they told me. I learned how to operate the lathe and shaper and, of course, the drill press, and to use a chisel and file to chip. They had me chipping days at a time. Very nice work and very interesting if you have an interest in that kind of work.

"There was an Englishman working there in the shop who had worked in India and every damned place and he was very kind to me. He would say, 'If you could just keep your mind off the bloody horses.' I would be looking out the window, watching farmers at their fall plowing. 'I could teach you something,' he'd say, 'but all you can think about is those bloody damn horses and cows.'

"I stayed there about a year, working in the shops. Then my mother went out to Ohio to visit my grandfather Osman. And as soon as she left I quit the shops and got a real job at real money; a dollar a day, driving for Adams Express.

Chapter 5

"WHEN I worked for the express company I made the trains and hauled cases and trunks for the drummers. And I might have stayed there, but I got sick. My mother being away, I ate out, and you know how a boy is about food. Since I was somewhat undersize I ate a lot, trying to get bigger. I would go to Bill Bacon's and have a fried-egg sandwich with onion and catsup on it. Then I'd have a fried ham sandwich with mustard on it. They were a nickel apiece. Then I'd go to the drugstore and have an ice-cream soda. And then a chocolate sundae. Then I'd go have a beer. I'd tasted beer before, but it was different to walk into a bar and order a beer and drink it right down. It was bitter at first but it didn't take me long to get to like it.

"Well, I got the bellyache, just downright bilious, so I quit that job and went to Bucyrus, Ohio, where my grandfather lived and where my mother was visiting. My mother wasn't very pleased to see me, and of course my grandfather said I had to get a job.

"You remember when McKinley was shot? When that happened I was working for Lafayette Yeagley. He was one of those fringe-whiskered Yankees and he was very thorough teaching me things, how to do good plowing, how to cut corn. He said that if I didn't cut but three shocks a day, he wanted them cut right. You pulled four stalks of corn together to make a little horse, you see, to set your corn around. You didn't use twine. You spliced cornstalks together. You stuck one end in the shock and walked around and pulled it together, tying it. A hundred and forty-four hills of that kind of corn, ten- and twelve-foot corn, was a lot of corn. There were professional corn cutters that would come with their knives and their appetites and cut for a nickel a shock and board. They made real wages, forty shocks a day at a nickel a shock. Why, two dollars a day without board was big money for a mechanic.

"Working on that farm is one of my pleasantest memories—there south of Bucyrus in the flat country on the Columbus pike. I slept upstairs and ate at the table with the Yeagleys. They had family prayers, morning and night, and all the help came in to pray and eat with them. When the hay balers were there there'd be Yeagley and his wife and three daughters—one of them waiting table—and three or four baler hands and myself. Same way threshing, except the whole damn neighborhood came. We had everything in the world that was good to eat, and crocks of milk and home-made pies. I worked for him all summer till the work was done and then I went to work in town.

"First I worked at the boarding barn, which was very nice. I'd bought a little mare of my own by then, and I worked at the boarding barn for her keep. They'd board a horse for eight dollars a month in a straight stall, and ten dollars a month in a box stall. That was real cheap, to feed and keep a horse up, wash the carriage, clean the harness and all.

"There was a doctor named Bryan who kept race horses, trotting horses, in a stable at the fairground. He'd have sales of surplus horses now and then, and there was one old stallion named L'Etoile that went at one of those sales for fifty dollars. He was nineteen years old and only had one eye and they said that he'd killed a couple of men but I think it was by accident, running away, that sort of thing. He was one of the most beautiful horses I ever saw, a beautiful head, just like an Arab's, and he was long and low and carried his head like a wild goose. I looked up his breeding and he had a right to be beautiful. His grandsire was Mambrino King, the most handsome horse there ever was, the greatest trotter and show horse of his day. You know, the one that pulled a buggy with two men in two-twenty on a half-mile track? Now that's moving. It just shows about blood. He sure was beautiful. *Muy caballo.*

"I'd like to have bought him myself but couldn't. And it is one of the few regrets of my life. An implement dealer bought him just to run on the snow path that winter. South Main Street on a winter Sunday afternoon was just devoted to harness horse races, in cutters. Anybody that had a horse that could move at all just went down there, circled back and forth and drove those blocks on South Main, right at half a mile, maybe, and you could pick up a brush with anyone that drove up alongside of you. A cutter is made for two people, made for speed. Shaped like a swan or bird, and some made very light and close-fitting. Well, that old fifty-dollar horse just cleaned up on the snow path that winter.

"I didn't do so well. I had this little mare of my own that I was working at the boarding barn to keep. A little Texas pony, we called them, and just as wild as hell. They used to bring them in there a carload at a time. Most of the horses around there, though, were standard, well-bred trotting horses. I both rode and drove my mare. I'd been reading *Sapho* and I called her Fanny LeGrand. And I had a little runabout. The fire chief had had it built for himself, but it was small and light and the old man outgrew it or got afraid to handle it. My grandfather Osman bought it and gave it to me, or let me use it. A very nice little rig, very well made, but I couldn't get any girls to ride in it. It was so tight. A hug seat—you know. And I didn't do any good on the snow path.

"One day I rode my mare out to the fairground track. Bill Ingram, the trainer, was working horses for Dr. Bryan, and he says, 'Boy, can that pony run?' I says, 'Yeah, she can run.' 'I tell you what you do. I'm working old Tibbicombe,' that was his pacing stud. 'I'm going to give him a mile. On the last quarter you wait for me at the quarter pole and pick me up there and make pace for me. I just want to see what he can do.'

"It was a half-mile track and I got down at the quarter pole with my mare. When Tibbicombe got even with me I turned that pony loose. She was running her damnedest, and that old stud came by me, whoosh. Before he got to the wire his nostrils were so wide open I could have shoved my two fists in there. I'll never forget the sound of his feet and his breath coming from behind, he-ragh, he-ragh, he-ragh, and he just passed my pony like she was tied. Old Bill setting up there, his derby hat pulled low over his eyes. He had his hands in the handloops and still he was holding a whip and stopwatch in his hands. He was a real driver, a driver from Giles, as we used to say in Arizona. I think he made that mile in two seventeen. On a half-mile track.

"I was always broke. Miss Keil, a cousin of my mother's and a lovely lady, used to give me a quarter to pump the big church organ for her to practice. It was fun. I would go to the little hat shop she owned, and she would loan me five dollars against my next payday. She knew that I would spend it riotously, but never a sermon did she make. Five dollars in those days insured an evening of real pleasure. Everything.

"I left the job at the boarding barn and got a job at the blower works. They made all kinds of fans, and I was in sheet-metal work. My grandfather was a friend of the manager, Jack Sheckler, who kept horses at the boarding barn. He had a fine buggy and fine driving horses. Fast, too.

"That was my first experience with a strike. There was quite a comical fellow working there, a regular monkey, and he was quite an agitator, too. He had it all figured out. Everyone, he'd say, was working too damn cheap. We'd just strike and then they'd have to pay us. He was a nice fellow, had very amusing ways of saying things, and of course I listened to him. I might have struck, I don't know. But Jack Sheckler, the manager, sent for me and said, 'Now see here, Kelly, you're just a boy. I know your grandfather and your people and you come from good stock to work. These fellows are going to walk out at noon and every damn one of them that walks out never comes back here to work again. I just thought I'd tell you because you're a young fellow.'

"Only a few of them walked out and they got sacked. There was a lot that thought they wanted to walk out but didn't when the time came. I always thought it was nice of him to tell me, because you know a boy can be influenced by jovial people and talked into doing anything just for the hell of it.

"Some time after that I got let out at the blower works and went back to work for old Porter, back at Scottdale, in Pennsylvania. I got better wages than before, and I was entrusted with a four-horse jerkline team to haul coal from the little drift mines to the lime kilns. And then spreading the lime on the land was a terrible job. You generally picked a windy day so it would go farther. It burned your eyes and your hands and it cracked your skin and it made you feel miserable. But of course all that went with being a man. They said you weren't a man until you could smoke real stogies and chew Wayman's tobacco. Boy, it was strong, and it looked like black corn silk. Or Freiberger's. It was all about the same.

"I am glad I was born when I was. A great pleasure, memories are, and I wonder if people today have as much pleasure in them. They have so little to remember. I was driving a jerkline team while I was still just a boy."

Chapter 6

ALL his life Kelly had a sharp and eager eye for landscapes and a hunger for new places. A half century earlier he would have been in the van of the great westward movement when it was still an adventure rather than the real estate industry it was rapidly becoming in his own day. Spiritually he was more akin to the plainsmen and the mountain men than he was to the practical, pious and self-satisfied farmers, mechanics and merchants of the East. As a child he had heard his elders speak often of the marvels of the New West. And as a young man he read hungrily of life on the Plains, the ease with which a man could get government land for farming or grazing, the geometrical progression with which herds of cattle grew in the new land and the richness of the sod, once cut and broken by the plow. Sometimes he dreamed of Texas but more often of Nebraska, which he remembered having seen distantly as a child when he had gone with his father to look at the cliff swallows' nests in the bluffs above the muddy Missouri. Beyond the great river lay a land where men still lived on horses, and this was a stronger lure than the prospect of quick and easy wealth.

He read eagerly of Fremont's explorations and devoured Parkman's *The Oregon Trail*, wishing that there might still be time to see "the prairies and the mountains before the irresistible commonplace subdued them." He studied the handbills and "newspapers" published by the Western railroads describing the lushness and desirability of the millions of acres of lands that bordered their rights of way in checkerboarded sections, the lands they would gladly sell at ridiculously cheap prices. He could, in time, recite paragraphs and pages of the improbable, seductive things that were being said about Nebraska.

The climate unexcelled. . . . The summer a long and genial warm season with delightful, breezy days and cool, refreshing nights; the winter mild and pleasant . . . the soft blue haze, subdued mellow sunshine and gorgeous red sunsets of autumn . . .

the rare, invigorating, life-inspiring atmosphere which gives remarkable brilliancy to the climate and leaves its impress upon every form of life. . . . The undying wind a true blessing, preventing stagnation of the air. . . . The water not only far beyond average in purity, but also abundant . . . the average annual rainfall steadily increasing due to the increasing absorptive quality of the soil brought about by increased cultivation by sturdy, God-fearing pioneers. . . . Grains and fruits and vegetables beyond man's dreams. . . . Unbelievable profits to be made in the rearing, fattening and sale of livestock . . . mild, nutritious grasses, fine water and cheap grain producing the best of stock at smallest expense. For climate, extent and value of pasturage, pure water, natural shelter, animal health and, indeed, everything that goes to make a perfect stock country . . . second to none on the face of the earth.

Kelly promised himself that as soon as he could get a little money ahead he would pack up and go to Nebraska to stay, buy a half-section of railroad land, homestead more.

His family moved from Pennsylvania to Elizabeth, New Jersey, where George Kelly was put in charge of the dismantling shops of the Central Railroad of New Jersey. They established themselves in a big, comfortable house at 1061 Mary Street on a pleasant, elm-bordered corner lot. Kelly followed them there from Scottdale and went to work first as a driver for an awning company—and lost his job because of his profanity, a natural outgrowth of his days in the harvest fields and the shops— and then for a hot-tempered German butcher named Schramm, who was more profane than Kelly would ever be. Finally he went to work again in the railroad shops and hated every minute of it.

He was now a working man. He drank beer at Gallagher's and at Joe McLaughlin's, headquarters of the Joe McLaughlin Society, an informal group of hard cases from County Kerry who ran the Irish-Democratic politics of Elizabeth. Kelly, for all his Protestant-Republican background, had an acceptably Gaelic name and was welcome to come through the side door on a Sunday morning to escape the clangor of church bells. Even more he liked Pat Turley's saloon, where the beer was cool and light in the summer, the ale and porter strong and comforting in the winter. It was a man's saloon, with wet mahogany, bright gleaming brass and the red eye of the stove shining in the gloom. Women might thrust a two-quart bucket, dime in the bottom, through the rear door, but were permitted to come no closer. The cheese on the free lunch counter was pale and sharp, and, when daubed with a little of the fiery mustard that Turley himself made, it could build an awesome thirst. So could the "mulligan" that Turley made and kept in a green hair tonic bottle on the bar, a stinging pepper sauce that regulars, Kelly included, would shake into their beer or ale to give it a bite. Years later Kelly was to try, unsuccessfully, to paint a picture of Turley's. He could not, he said, quite capture the peaceful solemnity of the place.

Kelly was happy to be together again with his brother Quill. Their best friend was Dave Hay, who lived five doors down the street. Dave's mother had been a schoolteacher, and the Hays' library was full of books that Kelly read hungrily. The three boys would often sit together at night and talk of books and girls and what they were going to do with their lives. Kelly would complain of the dirt and grease that no amount of scrubbing would remove from his hands and fingernails, and would swear that life would be different in the West. He would talk of the ranch he would, some day, own. Quill and Dave would come and stay with him. They would ride together across the rolling prairies and the hills, would round up cattle and survey the broad fields of grain, would swim in the broad, placid rivers and ride to town on Saturday nights. He would draw little pictures for them of how he imagined the West to be; often they were of men riding pitching horses, and more often than not the rider closely resembling Kelly himself.

Quill, eighteen months younger than Kelly, was bright and as happy in school as Kelly was out of it, as big and handsome as Kelly was undersized and plain, a fact that instead of jealousy inspired nothing but love and admiration in his elder brother. Quill worked hard at his studies, had won, at fifteen, a scholarship to Stevens Institute. He was an athlete and was, on occasional expeditions to New York with school friends, a hell-raiser. Wearing flat-brimmed derby hats, they toured side street saloons, they heckled John Alexander Dowie at his meetings and worked a fruitful sort of blackmail with Carrie Nation. They would escort the hatchet wielder into a saloon. While she was still in the preliminary or cigar-swatting phase of her attack they would negotiate with the management. Would it be worth while if they could persuade Carrie that there was a more iniquitous saloon, a hellhole more deserving of her attention, on down the street a way? It usually was. Even the great Tom Sharkey, who reputedly was so thrifty he cut his own hair, succumbed and set up champagne for Quill and his friends once they had led the frightening woman away.

Kelly enjoyed Quill's exploits vicariously. He took his own pleasure nearer home. He avoided, if he could, the social events of the Third Presbyterian Church, to which the Kellys belonged, preferring trips to the docks of Elizabethport with men from the shops for oysters and chowder, excursion steamers to Staten Island for clambakes, with all the food, beer and dancing you could handle for a dollar. Or the four-mile trip to Newark on pay nights, often with Ed Yoos.

"Ed was a curious-looking fellow, funny looking, you know. Big bulbous nose and black mustache. Black eyebrows that almost ran together. He looked cross but he wasn't. He was one of the funniest fellows I ever knew in my life. We'd go over to Newark, a much shorter ride than New York and just as much fun. We'd get box seats at Waldman's burlesque theater, right along next to the stage. They had waiters all over the house, carrying drinks. You drank right there and the air was full of smoke. Very few women went; the shows were quite rowdy, but very good. They'd have the ponies and the heavies, you know, as high as fifty girls. That was the first place I ever heard 'Good-by, My Lady Love,' a very beautiful old song. And the comedians were very amusing. Mostly Jewish or Irish, and then sometimes there'd be a big fat Dutchman. When the girls saw Ed and me sitting in the box and really taking an interest in the show they'd come and sing to us, right in front, you know. One time one of them was singing 'Come Down, My Evening Star,' and Ed took her at her word and started to climb over the railing, but I got him by the coattail and hauled him back.

"After the theater we always went to a Chinese restaurant and ate chop suey. I've always liked chop suey. And then sometimes we'd go to a house of entertainment. I don't know what street it was on but it was run by a Cuban woman, a beautiful woman. I had a girl there, a German girl and very lovely, and I used to go and see her when I could. It's funny, isn't it, that those girls are frequently damned pretty? Did you ever notice that? It always seemed kind of sad to me. Them being so bright and pleasant, you know. But then they were getting a little something out of life, and a lot of poor, decent working girls were not."

But for all the urban pleasures, Kelly still dreamed of the West. The dreams may have been inaccurate, but then so was much of the information on which the dreams were based. Propaganda of the Burlington and Union Pacific Railroads had, by this time, convinced him that his future was in a western Nebraska homestead, a little place in the sand hills.

Then Quill became ill. A doctor diagnosed it as exhaustion and incipient tuberculosis and advised a stay in a warm, dry climate. George Kelly consulted his eldest son. Quill had been studying too hard. Would Kelly take him to Arizona territory? Kelly didn't disillusion his father on the reasons for Quill's exhaustion, but willingly gave up his hope of going to Nebraska, at least for the time being. With Quill and a friend, Dick Bell, who had a similar lung condition, he boarded a train for a part of the world that was to be far more important in his life than Pennsylvania, Ohio and New Jersey could ever be. Their families had packed great quantities of food in a Gladstone bag. Because of washouts along the railroad line the trip to Arizona took two weeks, but the young men did not care. They stuffed themselves with food, told jokes, sang and waved at every girl they saw. Kelly played a harmonica and spent hours telling how the West would be.

Chapter 7

"MY dad had said, 'Wouldn't you just as soon go to Arizona with your brother? He doesn't know a thing about livestock and those kind of people. You're the elder brother, and I look to you to look after him.' You know, when he'd been in Arizona just a little while old Quill was six feet tall and weighed 180 pounds, and he was damn hard to look after. The Mexicans just loved him, and everyone called him Sour Ball Kelly. He was good-natured and when someone would start to get mad he'd say, 'Now don't get sourballed.' The Mexicans called me Chapo Kelly. That means little guy. I used to play the French harp for them.

"We all went to Prescott first. It was October and just as cold as billy-be-damned, there in the mountains. From Prescott we went to a mining camp, the Joe Mayer Mining Company. Just a post office and a robissary, that's what everybody called the company store, and the offices. Quill was supposed to get a job there through some friends of my father's, and I could have got on as a teamster, which was the only job I wanted and which paid well. But it was too damn cold and Quill got an attack of some kind of mountain fever. We remembered how pretty and warm it had been in Phoenix on the way up. Quill drew his few days' pay and we started out to walk eighty miles to Phoenix down the old Black Canyon Road. On foot. It was fifteen miles between freight camps, where the only water was, and us carrying our suitcases and bedrolls. We were green enough to think we might catch a burro and load our suitcases on him. Did you ever try to catch a burro? One of the fleetest damn animals in the world.

"It was all desert and we made it in four days. Dick Bell was with us, and he was really sick with his lungs. We'd start out each morning from the freight camp with canteens full of water, and after a while old Dick would begin to falter. We'd stop and rest and drink our water, and we'd usually run out before the day was half finished. Dick would say, 'I just can't go another step,' and we'd cuss him and pull him around and finally get him going again. It's a wonder we didn't kill him, sick as he was. Finally he just gave out. But ahead of us we could see the timber line of the first canal. That was in the New River Desert. So Quill and I left Dick and went ahead to this canal. We took off our shoes and soaked our feet in the clean, cold water coming from the mountains. We filled a bottle and took it back to old Dick and got him going again. That night we made a dry camp on the canal. That is, with no grub. Then the next day we went on into Phoenix and went to a wagon yard. That's where your work comes and goes. This one was called the Five Points Corral.

"We stayed there at the wagon yard a day or so, looking for work. I had a chance for a job as a freighter. Joe Salks had a contract freighting for the Tonto Basin job, and he had big Studebaker freight wagons with brakes on them like a trolley car. Then he had trailer wagons that were smaller. And he had a swamper to go with each team. Six-mule jerkline teams. He paid good wages, better than the ranches did: forty a month and board. But he'd just give you broke leaders. The leaders were work mules that had been broke, but the rest of the team would be just green broncs. You'd just throw them in there and trust to God and a good whip. You'd put six mules out, two by two, and that lead mule is a long way ahead of you. The driver sat on the near wheel mule. Then the swing team. I saw some of them with their legs all skinned up and I asked a driver how come those mules to be all peeled up that way. 'I'll tell you,' he says, 'the turns are so damned short on that canyon road that sometimes the swing team has got to work both mules on one side of the chain.' That's just a little too short for me, especially if it's a half-mile to bottom if you roll off. So I didn't take the job.

"Then we met an old prospector, an old Irishman named Nick. We were talking about buying a burro to pack our stuff on to go looking for work, and he had some burros. He said, 'Don't you boys fool around with a damn burro. People would think you're touched in the head. It wouldn't be right. It's all right for an old man to go creeping around with a damn burro, but not a boy.' That was all he had to say to us about burros, but he told us how to get out to a ranch where we could get jobs.

"It was one of the biggest outfits around there, the Bartlett, Heard Land and Cattle Company. They had eighteen sections under irrigation besides all the desert land they had. Their main crop was cattle, but they also raised alfalfa for the cattle. Also barley and wheat and milk cows. The iron was Lazy BH, and the headquarters was three miles south of Phoenix. Not far. Just right to come in a-horseback on a Saturday night. And boy, we came in, too.

"We hired out as teamsters, although Quill had never handled a team in his life, but we did all kinds of work. It was just a working man's paradise. They started you in at a dollar a day and board. Well, my God, you could get rich on that. You didn't need to spend anything, but of course we did, and I'll say this, we got value received. There were lots of fellows coming in there for those good wages. Lots of fellows out of Texas and they were the most likable fellows you ever saw. Out of McCulloch County and San Saba and Lampasas and around in there. A lot of them were on the move on account of the fence wars.

"They fed good there. That was the only cow ranch I was ever on where they had milk to drink. They had that green alfalfa and a cow just gave buckets of milk. They had rice or oats for breakfast with lots of milk. And big bowls of stewed raisins, they called them *uvas*. Prunes, dried apricots and apples, bacon and ham and lots of beef. They butchered a beef every week. The old blacksmith was given the honor of killing the beef each week because he had been an old buffalo hunter. He used a Sharps rifle.

"When you were working in the fields they'd send your lunch out to you on a hay rack, all covered with napkins and everything very nice. Pitchers of milk and boilers of coffee and nosebags for the horses. A pleasant picture, men and horses eating together.

"Quill got well right quick. He was assigned to the headquarters and I went to the upper camp. I'd hoped we'd be together so I could show him something about being a teamster. I never got to give any instructions on how to harness up or anything. He would take the harness all apart and put it on the horses piece by piece. The other hands stood around and laughed. Instead of getting mad, Quill would laugh right along with them and then they'd help him.

"Everything was fine. I helped put in close to a thousand acres of wheat that winter in one field, one whole section and part of another, on newly leveled land, irrigated. I leveled up a lot of land, too. The land wasn't really thickety, but the sand blows up around anything that grows and makes little hummocks. Mexican hands would cut this brush and I'd come along with a fresno and a slip scraper and cut the hummock off. Every one of them you cut had some kind of varmit in it. Little red lizards with a salmon-pink belly, and a dark blue one with a sky-blue belly, and Gila monsters and two kinds of rattlesnakes, sidewinders and old diamondbacks. Plenty of bull snakes, too, but just a world of rattlesnakes. It was beautiful country and you could see for miles."

October—First Monday

Goats in Corral

Chapter 8

"SOMETIMES on a Sunday the fellows would wrestle, free style, for amusement, but most of them were too big for me. Then there was this Californian that came there to work. We didn't like most Californians. They threw their weight around. They were native sons and let you know it. But this one was a nice fellow and a real man. He said, 'Don't nobody here ever box?' and I said I played around at it a little and we put on the gloves, although I wasn't within twenty-five pounds of his weight or his height either. Every time I hit him I'd have to leave the ground to do it, and the Mexicans were standing around yelling for me, 'Ay, Chapo, Chapo,' There's a lot of difference between boxing and fighting. I never in my life boxed with a fellow I was mad at. I don't think it's a good policy. Well, I took one of the damnedest beatings any boy ever took. He just beat the damn face off of me and I had to eat out of the side of my mouth for days. But I didn't mind because we were just boxing.

"There at the upper camp was a fine fellow named Clarence Casner. Good to animals and children and hands, very generous and not much of a talker. A big man with a big blond mustache. He creased his cigarettes, never wet them, and he'd ride around on his big sorrel horse—it took a big horse to carry him—with a little brown paper cigarette hanging from his lip, and I always thought he'd set his mustache afire but he never did. He had the pale eyes of blond people that live in hot countries, like steel drill points shining under his hatbrim. He was good-natured, though, and never even raised hell when we tore up his go-cart or jolt-ass as they called them, there in Arizona.

"There was this Monk Perry, a roustabout from around Lampasas, and he was damned well named. He looked like one and when he was drinking he acted like one. He'd bought a black-maned sorrel filly, and one Sunday he was going to break her to drive; said he might get a girl and want to take her buggy driving. He borrowed Clarence's jolt-ass and put a trip rope on the filly's forefoot for me to hold, so if she ran away I could throw her. They use those trip ropes breaking a horse to work and they can sure get you in a hell of a mess. So we started out. The filly was just a-trotting and Monk says, 'Look at her go, by God, can't she trot. Whoopee!' He was yelling and hollering and I was sitting scooched up, holding onto the trip rope, when we came to one of those old Indian irrigation ditches that are hard to see until you're right there. The filly jumped the ditch, and the cart went into it and stayed there and the filly went right on. I landed on the ground, and Monk went sailing right out of there after the mare, still holding the lines and yelling, 'Whoopee,' and the jolt-ass was just a pile of junk. We took what was left of it back to Clarence, and all he said was, 'I'll be damned. Now I'll have to ride my horse.'

"Monk was also the cause of me being lopsided now, this hunched shoulder I got. We went to Phoenix one Saturday night to have a good time and he got drunk right away. I kept trying to shoosh him down, and the more I did the wilder he got. We were out in the south part of Phoenix and he'd ride up to a place, hollering, 'Open up, you nigger sonsabitches.' Being a Texan, that was the worst thing he could think of. Then they'd turn the lights out. In those days if they turned the lights out you'd better leave before you get shot. That's always dangerous. And I said, 'They're closing up, Monk, let's go,' and he'd say, 'I don't give a goddamn, I'm a free Texan, open up.' But I finally persuaded him, and just as he was getting back on his horse a fellow steps out with a gun. This fellow was afoot and I began to feel pretty important. We had good horses and he was just a little whistlepate constable, I thought. So I said, 'Mister, just how far does your jurisdiction extend?' And he says, 'Young fellow, it extends all over Maricopa County and the territory of Arizona.' He must have been a ranger, you know, and I said, 'All right, we'll be good.' But old Monk, he'd been just reeling in his saddle, and about that time he kicked his horse and yelled, 'Goddamn the law,' and took off hell-calarup. That ranger ran for his horse and I took off after Monk. There was no use to tell him to turn on the steam. He had it turned on. I didn't try to see if the ranger was chasing us, but just rode as hard as I could.

"About halfway back to the ranch we had to cross Salt River. I was riding an Appaloosa horse, and right in the middle of that dry river bed that long-footed devil stumbled on a rock and I lit on this shoulder on one of those big boulders. I woke up there, kind of addled in the moonlight, and here came Monk, looking for me. 'Where the hell you at, Brother Kelly?' he shouted, and I said, 'Just setting here. My horse fell and I believe my shoulder's broke.' I couldn't tell you how I did it, but I got up behind Monk on his horse, with one arm and him drunk and no help at all. His pony was gentle and was just about run down, but Monk was rocking and reeling in the saddle, and he'd bump me and it would hurt this shoulder something awful. He was just damned near laying on me. I punched him in the ribs and told him to straighten up, that he had me almost pushed off the horse. 'Why,' he said, 'damn your soul to hell, ain't I letting you ride this horse for nothing? Have I got to get down and whip hell out of you?' I says, 'Yes, you have.' He climbed down and started at me and I just put my good hand in his face and pushed and he went flat. 'That's all right, Brother Kelly,' he says, 'you're welcome to ride now.' He was so comical and lovable he just couldn't make you mad.

"I didn't get my shoulder set. I just put my arm in a sling and went on working with my good hand. That's why she's a little crooked. And I got a cussing from the saddle boss. The horse came in the next day and the saddle wasn't hurt, but it was a company saddle, and the saddle boss, a bad-tempered Virginian, was mad. I guess if my shoulder hadn't been broke we'd have had a fight. No man's going to talk to me that way if there's anything I can do about it.

"Phoenix was a very pleasant town. I used to eat in a Japanese restaurant there, where they had a Chinese cook. The ranch hands used to say the chickens they served were really fighting roosters that had been killed in matches over in old town. If they were, it was the best fighting chicken I ever ate. And they raised their own vegetables, too, all very good.

"The red-light district was two blocks long. The front doors were never open, but there were red curtains at the windows with lights behind them. And all along were hitching racks where you could tie your horse. At the end of the row was a saloon. You could stop there and have a drink and then go out the back way. It was very nice, all paved with flat stones, and there was a pergola with vines growing over it. Then you'd walk back by the houses where the girls were, the back way. They'd have their back doors and windows open. They were all very pleasant. Never grabbed you or tried to pull you in or anything. Girls of all nationalities. There was a Japanese girl who wore little steel knives in her hair, and one time she ran after me, calling, 'Boy, boy,' and bringing me my spurs. I'd left them. Wasn't that nice? They weren't rowdy. They were all well behaved. There was a Texas girl that I liked very much, but if I overstayed my time she'd shoo me out because her sweetheart would come for her at midnight. He was a dealer at the Palace and got eight dollars for an eight-hour shift which was very good money. Before I left Arizona they got married and bought a little hotel of their own. That's a pleasant thing to think of, that she got a good break. So many of those girls never do.

"There was lots of gambling. The games were wide open, all day and all night and Sundays. The only time they ever closed was when old Hi Hooper died. He ran the Green Front, and they all closed for his funeral. The Green Front was a gambling house and saloon. There was a bar that went the length of the building, and over here were the games. Every kind you could think of, faro and monte and policy wheels and blackjack and then some kind of a big crap table that I never did understand. The gamblers were men that were well thought of, and so were the dealers. You'd see gold instead of chips piled up. We always got paid in gold. Everyone wore vests, the gamblers very fancy ones. They were handy for the pockets, and no one wore a coat. A cowman, when he came to town, always rolled up his coat and tied it on the back of his saddle. When he got to town he'd put it on as a mark of respect to civilization and ladies. Then if he went to gambling he'd sit in his vest.

"Times when the river got up and we couldn't go to Phoenix maybe we'd go to Tempe. A quiet little town, you know, with no district. One of the few diversions was a barbershop where the barber's daughter did the shaving. She wasn't pretty or anything but some of the fellows liked to go there just so they could say they'd been shaved by a woman.

"There was this fellow at the ranch we called Pennsylvania Steve. He was a funny little dried-up Dutchman that spoke in a squeaky voice, but he was a freighter and teamster from Giles. I don't know if there really is a Giles or where it is. It's just some sort of Southwestern idiom, and it means very good, like you was to say I was a horse buster from Giles.

"Steve spoke just perfect Spanish and seeing he was so old we used to say he came to that country right after that old Spaniard, Cabeza de Vaca. He had a Mexican girl in Tempe that lived there with her family, and we'd go with him to call on them. She'd make tortillas and toast them for us and she and her whole family would chatter away at Steve in Spanish. It was very nice. Did you know that Mexican women dye their hair with *chapote*, that little wild persimmon, to give it that red-black color?

"This one time when the river was up we were in Tempe together and Steve asked me if I wanted a girl. I said sure, and he went out looking and pretty soon he came back to the saloon and told me to follow him. I did, through one dark little street after another, all the houses just alike, made of tules and 'dobe. It was pretty spooky, and all I could think of was tales I'd heard of people getting knifed by Mexicans. Finally we got to this house that was just like all the rest, and Steve shoved me in.

"She was very hospitable and pleasant and everything seemed all right until there was a noise from under the bed and I liked to jump clean into the street. She came running after me crying '*gallina, gallina,*' meaning hen. She had chickens under the bed. I was right nervous, there in the dark, and I gave her what I thought was a fifty-cent piece. It wasn't until some days later that I felt in my pocket and found I still had that fifty-cent piece, and that what I had given her was a good-luck piece that said: 'It's hell to be broke.'

"The next time I was in Tempe I tried to find her house to give her the money, but I never could, and by that time Steve had moved on someplace else.

"It's funny how when you get along a little in years you can remember things like that in detail, things that aren't at all instructive. And the useful things just slip your mind.

"We put up hay in May, and oh, they had fine haying tools. It was haying on a big scale, just a continuous performance. I'd never seen anything like it and I enjoyed it and should have stayed there. It was a good place and I might have had a future.

"But we took a notion to go, Quill and me. Everybody was talking about going to Oklahoma in those days, what the Texas fellows called 'up in the Nations.' Nobody talked about going or wanting to go to California. California had a hard name among working men. But they said there were lots of opportunities in the Indian Territory, fellows getting rich making crops on that good Indian land, some fellows even marrying wealthy Indian girls. Just like people in Missouri talking about all that rich land over in Arkansas. Anyway, we wanted to see Oklahoma, and we did. We had plenty of money to get away, but Quill met a girl bucking roulette and he disappeared for a while and when he got back we didn't have as much money as before. But we still had some and we started anyway, wearing fancy new boots, I remember. For Oklahoma."

Chapter 9

"OH, I've had some noble times. Riding into town, horses padding in the dust, spurs and spade bits jingling, girls calling, 'Hello, cowboys.' A couple of hours' sweat, the old bean cleaned up and another Saturday night in the offing. New countries to explore, new jobs to get the hang of and new friends to find. Then, move on. Sack the saddle and hit the rattler.

"When we were leaving Arizona we still had enough money left, even after Quill's spree, that we could have bought train tickets for Oklahoma, but that seemed like a useless way to squander money. We'd rather do it our own way. So we rode freight trains, paying each brakeman a dollar to let us ride his division. We'd stop in towns, buy steaks and other good things to eat, lay up in the hobo jungles and cook for ourselves, living high and moving slowly and spending more money than if we'd just bought tickets and gone on through.

"A colored fellow came in the jungle one night, a barber going from California back to Texas where his wife was dying. He had a message calling him home. Most brakemen, in those days, all you had to do was show them a message like that and they'd let you ride their freight without molestation. But this old boy was hungry. He'd gone into a restaurant in town. 'I got money,' he said, 'but soon's I stuck my head in the door a man throwed a cup at me, and before I could get turned around he slang his plate at me, too.' Ain't that a hell of a way to treat a man? Any man. We were sorry for him and gave him some steak and he stayed the night with us. I hope he made it all right.

"We got as far as Deming, New Mexico, and it was hard to get out of there. They were shipping cattle out of there for Denver and Colorado Springs from the Three C outfit, that's a big outfit, and we got jobs riding the trains and poking the cattle. We'd been better off if we'd just gone on beating our way, but the idea of managing a trainload of cattle apiece appealed to us. Travel like kings, boss of your own train.

"So we hung around Deming for ten days, waiting for the trains to be loaded and made up, just so we could travel like kings. We were low on money, too, by that time. You know how careless a boy is with money. We lived on stale bread and candy and slept in a haystack at the edge of town. There was no entertainment except for a murder trial. A rancher had killed a Mexican hand and they were trying him for it, but it was a joke. They had this Mexican woman that the dead man had boarded and roomed with, an older type woman. They'd ask her questions in Spanish. I could understand some of it and I heard her say, 'Only as a mother, señores, only as a mother.' And the judge and the jury just laughed and slapped their legs and stamped their feet. They turned that rancher loose and afterward he took everyone out and bought them drinks. We didn't go, Quill and I.

"But they had beer for us down where we were helping to load the cattle. There were big three-year-old steers with heavy horns, and a couple of cars of yearlings. They were being overloaded and overcrowded and they were snuffy anyway from the way they were being handled. They'd run them in the loading chute, and one old boy would swing up on the overhead brace and rowel those cattle from ears to tail with his spurs and holler and hoot, all to make them move faster.

"My train was finally loaded and I got my papers and lantern and loading pole. Every time the train stopped I'd take my loading pole and inspect every car to see if any of the cattle were down or getting trampled. The conductor was an overbearing old bastard and gave me a hard time about everything. One time I was working with the pole trying to poke a fallen steer back onto his feet. The steer kicked the pole and the other end of the pole like to knocked my head off. I got up off the ground, trying to get my senses back, and this old bastard was standing there, shouting at me, 'Ain't you ready to go yet?' I told him to get the hell on back to the caboose and chew his tobacco, and I'd be back when I was ready for the train to move. You see, if you've got a trainload, it's your train. That's what I mean by traveling like a king. That train won't move until you say so.

"After that I just took all the time I could inspecting the cattle, whether there was trouble or not. Of course lots of time there was trouble. One old steer got down and I couldn't get him back up with the loading pole in any damn way, shape or form. There was nothing to do but get in there and heave him up. There was a little square door high up in the end of the car, and I climbed in there, the steers all staring at me red-eyed. I got ahold of this fellow and got him up and just when I did he whirled to hit me. I made a leap for that little door and caught hold of the brake staff, and as I did he just went 'chumpff' and his horns hit the wall on both sides of my legs. He'd have broken them like pipestems. Those devils were really snuffy. After a cow brute's been punished and mishandled a while he really gets mad.

"Quill was on a train twenty-four hours behind me. We'd agreed that if we didn't get together in Denver we'd meet in Dalhart, Texas, which was in the direction we were heading. And we'd leave messages for each other there.

"Well, we rattled along and aside from keeping the cattle up and the conductor off of me the only thing I did was get off the train at Alamogordo and buy a bottle of beer for a dollar, which was a day's wage some places and two days' wages in others. It was good, though, even if it left me with only two dollars to my name. We were supposed to get paid when we got to Denver.

"I'd ride and sleep in the lookout of the caboose, which is very nice, you know. You can see the country all around you. One morning I woke up, up there, and oh, I thought I was in the most beautiful country I had ever seen. Rolling green grassland as far as you could see. Here and there a windmill, and a few cows way off yonder. And the bluest skies, with just a few little fluffy clouds. It was just sunup, and you know how beautiful the world is anyway at sunup, with the colors richer and the air cleaner. Beautiful any time but more so when you're just twenty years old. After being in the desert and the mountains it was just an entirely new world. I thought maybe I'd been dreaming and had woke up in Nebraska.

"So I hollered down to the conductor—I had a good conductor by then—and I said, 'Where in the devil are we at?' And he said, 'We're just pulling in at Dalhart, Texas.'

"When the train stopped I got out on the platform and stretched and breathed that good air. I saw an old boy just standing there, looking wishful. And I said, "Would you like to go to Denver?' And he said, 'You're damn right. I'd like to go up there and see my sis.'

"'Well,' I said, 'here, your name is Kelly now,' and I gave him my papers and told him where to find the loading pole and the lantern and how he'd really have to keep an eye on the cattle, overloaded as they were. He didn't get it at all, he was just in such a hell of a hurry to get on up there to Denver and say howdy to his sister. You could see that he was just a straight rambler.

"I bought me some socks and had a good breakfast and went to the blacksmith's shop and had a job inside of two hours, on a ranch. I wrote a postcard to Quill and left it there at Dalhart, telling him where I'd gone. Then I went out and worked on this ranch at only eighteen dollars a month, but the country was so beautiful that I didn't mind. After a while I got a card from Quill. Somehow he'd ended up in Amarillo. People had told him of all the opportunities there, and he'd got a job washing dishes in a café. Nights. In this Amarillo café. We both worked a while, long enough to get a road stake for our trip into the promised land. Oklahoma.

"Then after a little while I went down to Amarillo to collect Quill. We camped out in an empty barn. It was way up in June and quite pleasant. We set a day for our departure, but on the night before Quill didn't come home from his job as night dishwasher in that café. Come daylight I went to the café, and the day man was there from the day before, just madder than hell.

"'Old Big Boy,' he said, meaning Quill, 'never showed up, nor the night cook either, and I'm still on. They're both of them in the do-right, for disturbing the peace and drunk. They was playing coon-can and your brother got to feeling right good. He quit the game about even but stayed around, taking nips and feeling better and better. There's a new gambler in town and he was in the game and trimming the night cook. Cheating. Old Big Boy saw him at it and called him and then just beat the daylights out of him. The law came and old Big Boy lit out, hollering and whooping and kicking on doors, but the law caught him and put him in jail.'

"I went down there to the jail, a little old red-orange sheet-iron building and there was Quill with his face at the window, looking awful and saying, 'For God's sake get me out of here,' and the others guys in the jail shouting, 'Get the drunk sonofabitch out of here so we can get some sleep.' I went to see the judge, and he said, 'Well, you're just boys. He can lay here for trial next month, or he can plead guilty and I'll levy the smallest fine I can,' which he did. The fine was only one dollar, but the costs were ten dollars and seventy cents and I reckon that helped them along with the new courthouse they were building. There in Amarillo. It sure cut into our road stake.

"So we went out and had a good breakfast of fried liver and bacon and stacks of hot cakes with butter and sugar-cane sirup. I never ate such a breakfast in my life, for a quarter, anyway. I think the owner took pity on us and gave us extra portions. After that we felt better.

"We bought tickets and rode the cars because we figured it cost less than beating our way, at least the way we did it. We came into Indian Territory by way of Quannah and we got work shocking oats on a fine farm at Paul's Valley.

Chapter 10

"THE owner of the farm at Paul's Valley was a nice old man, and he asked us how come we came to Oklahoma. We said we wanted to marry some rich Indian girls, and he just smiled. We found out later he was married to a pure-dee Indian woman, and rich, too. But he was very nice to us and asked us, later, if we wanted to stay there and put in wheat on halves in the fall. That's the finest way there ever was for a fellow to get started farming. But it seems like every time we had a fine opportunity like that something always happened.

"We worked from sunup to sundown, in the oats. Those were heavy oats, a little short in the straw but heavy, about seventy bushels to the acre, and the sun would go down just so far and then hang there in the sky.

"This old man had a Canadian there on the farm as manager, and we didn't get along with him. He dealt in real estate on the side, leasing land from Indians at six bits an acre and leasing it out at two dollars and a half. People like that had the land all grabbed up, and that didn't make us like him any better.

"We slept on the porch and just got et up by those old striped leg gallinipper mosquitoes that could bite right through a quilt. And you'd drink that old wiggle-tail water. When you'd draw the coffeecan up out of the dug well for a drink it would be covered with wiggle-tails and you'd just have to blow them back. I got to having chills, and in between having chills and getting bit by the bugs I got to going into the kitchen nights to visit with an old long-legged swarthy Texas girl the Canadian had there as cook. That fellow came in one night and caught me, and I gave him the rought side of my tongue. Then Quill came in, swatting mosquitoes and cursing and ready for a fight, and he lit into him too, and the next morning we got our checks and went our way.

"Oh, we saw a lot of beautiful Indian girls with shining hair and pretty teeth, but they wouldn't even look at us, let alone marry us.

"We went up through Oklahoma City and on up to Nelagoney and Pawhuska in the Osage country. They were tapping that oil country and running oil down Bird's Creek, killing the fish and every other damn thing. They didn't have slush pits and they were wasting that much oil. The Indians in there were rich even before oil was found. They'd come to town driving matched spans of fine horses with silver-mounted harness and Studebaker surries with fringe tops and rubber tires. And no matter how many there were in the family the old copper-colored daddy rode up in front, alone, and everyone else was in the back. Bacon Rind was chief then, a wonderful smart man.

"On the Fourth of July we saw a horse race there in the Osage country. The Indians came from all over, lots of them old-timers wearing nothing but a gee string and a blanket. They all sat on the ground and they bet everything on the races, blankets, saddles, ponies, money. Wagons and hacks were all up and down each side of the little quarter-mile straightaway race course. There were white fellows there, too, with horses, ranchers and professional quarter-horse men. Some fellows rode in long drawers and sock feet. If they wore drawers at all in those days, they'd be long ones, out of light cotton.

"There was a big fine-looking gray one-eyed horse. You've got to watch one-eyed horses. They'll always bear a little to the blind side. They're like my ear. I can hear only on one side and I'm not oriented. You can holler at me, and I don't know where in hell you're at. And this old horse, this one-eyed horse, just flew the track and knocked Indians end over end and ran through and tore up a couple of damn surries. Some of those big old dignified whey-bellied Indians just scooted out of there on their all-fours, and all a-laughing.

"We went to work, then, out from Pawhuska where they were building the railroad, working for a real old-time hard-boiled railroad contractor named Lindsay Kincaid. The kind of sonofabitch that wore red flannel underwear in Oklahoma in July, a red flannel undershirt with a white dress shirt over it and the sleeves rolled up and no collar, but always with a vest and a derby hat. In that heat.

"His straw boss was Blackie O'Neil. Blackie was out on three-thousand-dollar bail for bringing whisky into the territory to sell to the Indians. That was a federal offense and a bad one. And next under Blackie was Forty-Eight. He was a paroled convict and that was his number as a convict, and that's all anyone every called him. He and Blackie were as likable and as trustworthy fellows as I've ever known.

"But Quill didn't like Blackie, and neither one of us liked Kincaid or the work either. I was working with a slip in a mud cut. In my team I had one of the coldest-jawed mules I ever handled. If you wanted to turn her, you'd drop one line so you could get both hands on the other one and then just set your feet and pull. All that iron-jawed mule would do, she'd open her damn mouth and get her chin set against her neck and keep right on going. Working in a mud cut is bad enough anyway, slipping and sliding around, without having to fight a mule that is half alligator.

"Whatever Quill was doing he wasn't hitting it off. It was hot and muggy, and we slept in tents with mosquitoes biting us and bull snakes and pissants and every other damn thing creeping and crawling on us, and we just plain wanted to quit. But we'd heard that we'd have trouble with Kincaid, collecting our wages due. He wouldn't pay off until his regular payday, they said. I guess that way he protected himself from floaters and ramblers. One fellow had quit already and when he asked for his money Kincaid peeled his head with a pistol butt and ran him off without a penny. The fellow came back that night and took the taps off all the wheel scrapers and threw them away to get even. Kincaid had him run down and thrown in jail and that didn't make us like him any better.

"We weren't going to be treated that way, and Quill said, 'We ain't any damn paupers. Let's get us a lawyer.' So we talked to this lawyer, and the lawyer talked to the Indian agent—the Indian agent was always the stud duck in those places, and then he told us that Kincaid would pay us off, all right, even if it wasn't payday.

"We went to Kincaid's tent and he had an old-time high bureau in there and on top of it was a frontier model Colt, a single action peacemaker. He gave us our checks and then said, 'Now get out of here goddamn fast.' I moved so fast that I tromped on Quill's feet and he said, 'Aw hell, take your time. We ain't in no hurry.' He didn't see the gun, but he wouldn't have given a damn if he had. He wasn't afraid of the devil, I'll say that for him. I'll tell that to anyone, and I'll tell it on Judgment Day.

"It took all we collected from Kincaid to settle with the lawyer, and a little bit more. So we started north for Kansas. On foot."

Chapter 11

"NOW I've been broke most of my life and I guess I'll always be broke, but the only time I was so bad broke that I was hungry was up there in Kansas. We really hit poverty row there. Really honest-to-God hungry. We beat our way and we walked and we covered lots of ground, up in around Coffeyville and Yates Center and all up in there. It was a beautiful country and a good year. There were trees along the road just loaded with the best wild cherries you ever tasted, just hanging over the fence. And orchards bent down with good apples. Grimes Golden. All kinds. We'd go to a bakeshop and get a baker's dozen of sweet rolls, buns, for a dime. They'd almost always give you thirteen. And you could get a pound of cheese for a dime. But then we ran out of dimes.

"We'd walk along and we'd ask for work, but it was after harvest and prairie haying hadn't started yet. And we just didn't have anything except I had my French harp and Quill had some chewing tobacco, but I can't chew tobacco when I'm hungry, so we went along eating wild cherries and apples. You try making a breakfast on wild cherries and apples sometime. And then start out on the road. You know.

"One Sunday we hit it lucky. An old man with a long white beard and two nice-looking young ladies were sitting on the porch of this farmhouse. I asked them if there was anything we could do around there to earn something to eat. Just a bite to eat. 'No, boys,' said one of the girls, she was like a Biblical character, 'there's no work because this is Sunday, but we'll give you something to eat.' And she went in and got us a big old gallon pitcher of sweet milk, a plate of light bread and butter, and a big crock of applesauce. While we were eating the other girl came and just stared at us and didn't say anything. Just stared. I guess they were sisters, but the other one treated us like human beings. We weren't tramps. We weren't dirty or anything. Just boys.

"That was about noon. We hit the road again, and by evening we were back on wild cherries and apples. We sat under a tree and Quill said, 'Harry, get out the French harp and give us a tune.' So I played 'Soldier's Joy,' which some people call 'Hell Among the Yearlin's' and others 'Pissants March on the Sugar Bowl.' It's an old fiddle tune, good for when you're feeling droopy.

"And Quill said, 'Do you know what they had to eat today at 1061 Mary Street, Elizabeth, New Jersey?' That's where our folks lived. 'They had a big pot roast with brown gravy and potatoes all around it, and no telling what in hell else, probably pineapple sherbet for dessert. Play us another tune on the French harp.'

"And we started out the next morning again, full of wild cherries and apples and pep. 'Long toward evening we came to a little house, and I told Quill I was tired fronting for us, that he had to do it this time. It's embarrassing, you know. Quill marched up there and a little old lady came to the door. 'Good evening, ma'am,' Quill said, and sort of bowed. 'Lady,' he said, 'we been a-marching and a-jungling and to tell you the truth we're hunting work.' She said, 'Well, I don't have any work,' and Quill went right on blarneying her, never mentioning what we really needed was food. So I said, 'We'd like to know if there is anything we can do to make our supper. Any chores or anything. We can do anything.' She said there wasn't, but invited us to sit down and she'd get us something to eat.

"I remember, she brought us fourteen cold homemade biscuits and a pitcher of cold milk and another damn crock of applesauce. When we got through we thanked her and she said, 'I'm glad to feed you boys. I've got a boy out away from home and I don't know where he is or what he's doing.' And I said, 'Well, I know one thing for sure. God's seeing to it that he eats.' There were lots of boys like us on the road in those days—not hoboes or bums, just restless boys.

"The next morning we had our breakfast of wild cherries and apples and hadn't gone very far when a man came by driving a beautiful pair of horses, a gelding and a mare. They were Cleveland bays, if you've ever seen them. A tall horse bred by the English as a coaching horse. Quite a few were brought to this country in the nineties, but they were never liked much here because they were too leggy and we already had trotting horses that would beat anything on the road. And we had fine draft horses and didn't need any more general-purpose horses. The only general-purpose horses that fit in America were the Morgans in New England and the quarter horses here in the Southwest. At that, they were nice, really beautiful, and I was admiring them when he stopped. He was driving them to a hack and had fly covers on them, and one of the check reins was loose. He had a very heavy accent and asked if I'd rein his horse for him, which I did. While I was doing it we hit him for jobs. He said he could use me in a day or so when he started on his millet hay, and he said my brother could get a job on down the road at a neighbors' who was going to start with a hay baler soon. I guess he wanted me because I admired his horses so much. He told us how to get to his place, a mile this way and a mile that, and we'd see two red barns and a stone house.

"Well, that stone house was just like back in Ohio and Pennsylvania, and it made me feel good just to see it. His wife took me in and set me down to some cold fried eggs with bacon chopped up in them and some buttermilk and honey and sirup and butter and everything in Christ's world a man would want to eat. I tried to control my appetite but I guess I was stuffing and shaking and she asked me if I hadn't had my dinner. I said, 'No, ma'am,' and she asked me when I'd eaten last. I said, 'Last night,' and you know, tears came to that woman's eyes.

"Her husband's name was Ulrich Wagner and he was Swiss. He had the nicest house, and he'd built it with his own hands. The parlor was wainscoted with first one board of maple and then one of walnut, all off his own place. He had homesteaded eighty acres and bought another eighty and he had a perfect farm. Good fertile land, and he had taken care of it. He was the hay-makingest damn man I ever saw in my life. He raised more millet to the acre and he had modern haying equipment and it was just hotter than the hinges of hell down in the Neosho River bottom. No wind at all. It was one of the nicest places I ever worked, and I worked harder. Every morning in the fields he'd come out and give me a big tin cup half full of white wine that he made himself, and the same in the middle of the afternoon. I never drank more than half of what he brought me, but he never brought any less. It made me feel good, that he'd do that.

"On Sundays, Quill would come to eat with us. The farm where he was didn't feed very good. And before dinner Ulrich would bring out the tin cup full of wine and hand it to me. I'd drink just a little and then hand it to Quill and he would finish it, then just laugh and talk during dinner. After dinner we'd sit under the little grape arbor and Ulrich would tell us stories about Switzerland and France and Germany and how he had liked to go to the 'shock-a-lot houses.' And he would smoke his weekly cigar. Just one a week. When it got short he would stick a toothpick in it and smoke it until there just wasn't any left.

"After I left Quill came and worked for Ulrich a while, before going back to New Jersey. Quill was very willing but he didn't know much about farming. Ulrich would send him out to bring in the cows for milking. Quill would say, 'How many cows?' Ulrich would say eight cows. So Quill would go to the end of the lane and turn in the first eight head. They were all fine cattle. It would be dusk by that time and the old man would be out there with his milk pail calling, 'Sug, Dewey, sug, Dewey.' All his cows were named for admirals and generals. Then he'd cuss in German and say, 'That ain't Dewey, that's a steer.' That just shows you how harum-scarum, happy-go-lucky Quill was. He was a willing hand, though, if you told him what to do.

"Ulrich wanted me to stay there with him, but I still had Nebraska on my mind, and if ever I want to see anywhere, why I'll be bound to go, and if I ever live I don't know but what I'll see Spain yet. So I went up to Nebraska then, and I got up there in time to see the state fair at Lincoln. I've always liked fairs. Old Bull-dog Pickett was there. Do you remember him? Or hearing of him? He would catch a steer by the horns, from his horse. Then he'd throw himself over onto the steer's back and lean over between the steer's horns and get the steer's nose in his teeth and throw him. Just like a bulldog.

"And they had a harness-broke longhorn steer there named San Antonio Pete. That old steer trotted to a sulky a mile in three minutes. I really enjoyed that.

"Oh yes, and William Jennings Bryan was there, too, but I didn't pay him no mind. It wasn't that he was a Democrat. I voted for him in 1908. It was just that I never did care much for speeches."

Chapter 12

THE crystal and opal of the desert, the starkness of the pine-draped mountains and the dry tableland, the thick grass of the High Plains waving in the unending wind, oil flowing from the ground in the Indian Nations, rich hayfields and orchards and corn in Kansas—all these Kelly had stored in his mind, alive and rich in color. Still he was eager for more. Nebraska was the country he had dreamed of and Nebraska he must see. Now on freight cars, now on foot, he wandered through the state, sleeping in livery stables and empty barns. He saw the stockyards of Omaha, the fine displays of grains and fruits and cheese and fat cattle and swine at the state fair, the seemingly boundless prairies, yellow now in the fall of the year. He would stop and talk to homesteaders of their experiences, listen eagerly to their tales of fat, profitable offers for relinquishment of the land they had settled. He saw dummy claims where great cattle companies had built shacks in the names of their cowhands to keep homesteaders off the range. He stopped and helped men who were cutting heavy sod into long strips and rolling it up like carpeting to build the walls of a prairie house. The wide, sandy rivers would rise with the rains and then, falling again, leave fish stranded in a thousand muddy pools. The provident settlers would come with shovels and tow sacks, scoop up the fish and take them home to be salted down in barrels. They would help feed the big haying crews next year.

Hungry and out of money, Kelly stopped and worked for part of the fall and winter for a sheep-feeding ranch on the Republican River. Range-lean wethers, ewes and lambs were brought by the thousands from Wyoming. Grazing first on stubble and then on harrowed-down corn, they would learn to eat grain and hasten their own end. Controlled by a dog that knew more about sheep than a man could, they lived in panel corrals and spent their days in gluttony, feasting on alfalfa, shell corn, spelts and barley, doubling their weight in ninety days before going off to the yards in Omaha where they would bring, in pennies per pound, twice what they had brought on the windy ranges of Wyoming. Kelly was impressed. He learned the strange, hysterical ways of sheep. He broke mules and helped with the grain crop that would feed the sheep. When the sheep were taken away to the yards he helped dismantle the corrals, spread the thick-packed manure in the grain fields, plowed, drilled and harrowed.

Kelly loved the country and was fired with ambition. He wrote to his old friend, David Hay, with all the fervor of a railroad propagandist.

"The happy country life is so far ahead of the city with its crowding, pushing mobs. On Sunday to walk around the place, your hands behind your back with a feeling of solemn joy and contentment, and in the afternoon a drive around the country with always something new and beautiful to draw your attention. I thank the Almighty we have the love of these things in us, so as our minds are not always full of unworthy plans and plots.

"This country can't be beat for climate. The nights are cool and the mornings frosty. Such a fine, bracing, dry atmosphere, and the cold just keeps a fellow's blood moving. The air is clear and the sun warm and bright and I can look for miles north toward the Platte, where I intend to ride one of these days. There's plenty work up there, prairie haying and also cow-work on the ranches. It is now cow country, but the covered wagons going north tell the story of farms and schools and churches up that way, and we all must get our land there soon. There's government land to be had north of the Platte on the divide, level tableland. There's a chance for us all together to take up adjoining claims. We could all live together and tell tales of our travels in the thickening smoke. I won't rest until we all, our folks and yours, are settled in the West. Like the Bible says, 'But they shall sit every man under his vine and under his fig tree; and none shall make them afraid.' For stock I like the Shorthorn for a farm or the Hereford for the open range and hard rustling. Among sheep I like the Hampshire (that is in cultivated country); for range sheep I care little. Of hogs I, like most Nebraskans, favor the Duroc-Jersey. He is a wizard to rustle and the sows sure raise good-size families and are superior in that way to the Poland China. Of fowls I like the S. C. B. Leghorns, the Pekin ducks and the Mammoth Bronze turkeys. Geese I don't like. And last but not least, ladies, *all* of them. Once I make a claim here I'm going to make a visit back to New Jersey where they grow *girls*.

"Tonight as I came from the barn I saw a flock of ducks cutting sharply against the red of the evening sky and thought of you, the mighty hunter. The little cottontails are plentiful on the prairie and in the corn, as well as their big sleek cousin, Jack. The quail and prairie hens are my favorites, though I do not hunt. I like to watch them, neat and brown and busy. I am anxious for spring to hear the prairie roosters crowing in the green buffalo grass and the tall bluestem.

"You must learn to ride. Just to pile a big stock saddle on a prancing pony and go off feeling like you were astride a comet. Go tearing into the village of a Saturday night, go clanking and jangling about in spurs, soft hat and neckerchief. There's nothing like a horse. To go snorting and pitching along the line makes a fellow's blood feel like it does when he sashays around to the tune of 'Turkey in the Straw' or 'Arkansaw Traveler.' I guess I'm kind of a queer fellow. Sometimes I feel ornery and full of mischief as a yearling mule, and nothing but racing the ponies will satisfy me, and again I feel as meek and quiet and solemn as an old bellwether.

"I've nothing much more to say only that the mules kicked me clear and clean out of the barn over on the section where I was before. We'd butchered a hog and they smelled blood.

"You'd better come out to Nebraska in the spring. We boys will start in and lead the simple life in a sod house and hunt ducks on the prairie lagoons and trap coyotes and gray wolves in the bluffs and canyons. It's kind of an uphill fight out here alone, but we'll soon be together in the green springtime."

He saved some of the twenty-five dollars he made each month and was eager to move on to the more open country, the sand hills and beyond.

The owners of the ranch on the Republican liked him, wanted him to stay. They hinted that they might, in time, give him a financial interest in the operation. But the urge to move on could not be denied. He joined a wagon train as a mule skinner and moved on toward the West, bound for a town he had never heard of and which, afterward, he could never remember, for he never got there. He left the wagon train in Cheyenne. In the convivial atmosphere of a saloon he learned that Campstool Ranch was in need of hands. And he met a young man from Illinois who had, as he had done somewhat earlier, come West to find, at best, his fortune, or, at least, some fun. He wore a business suit, a long overcoat and a pair of fringed buckskin gauntlets just like those worn by Buffalo Bill Cody in his Wild West show. He was greatly impressed with Kelly's knowledge of the West, and Kelly enjoyed divulging it. The boy confessed that he had spent the last of his money on the buckskin gauntlets and a red silk kerchief. Kelly loaned him enough money to pay his hotel bill, and together they boarded a Union Pacific train which would drop them at the siding nearest the Campstool Ranch on Cow Creek.

They stumbled through the deep snowdrifts to the ranch headquarters and were met by a short-spoken Irishman named Conroy, who, it appeared, was the boss of the cattle operation. Conroy listened while Kelly told him of his own experience and stared in disbelief at the yellow gauntlets, silk kerchief and long overcoat of the boy from Illinois. He told them their first job would be to skin some dead cows in the corral. Kelly sharpened some knives, examined the stiff bodies of the cows enough to know that they were thawed on the surface. He went to work, slitting them down the bellies and the legs and around the neck and used a horse to peel the hides away from the frozen flesh. His companion stared, turned green and walked back to the railroad siding. Kelly never again saw him or the money he had loaned him. Nor cared. The next day having proven his willingness to take on a menial and distasteful job, he was issued a saddle and heavy clothing and began riding the range.

Spring seemed never to come to Wyoming, and day after day he rode in sub-zero temperatures in the months when the days grew longer and the cold only seemed to become more intense. On infrequent days off he would ride into Cheyenne for a relaxing evening and there he bought a saddle of his own from Frank Meanea, who was, he always said later, a saddlemaker from Giles. In the bunkhouse on the short Sunday afternoons he would play his French harp while the other hands sang and stomped out impromptu dances. He was a trusted hand and soon became Conroy's top lieutenant.

Chapter 13

"AT the time I thought of Conroy as an old fellow. He was about forty-five or so and he had been riding since he was fourteen. I sure didn't want to spend my life the way he had his. I thought: By the time I'm an old man like that I'll have a place of my own. He wasn't even foreman, but that was because they didn't have a foreman for the cattle operation on the Campstool; just for the sheep. He was just sort of the stud duck for the cattle handling. He was getting pretty stiff and would have to fight his horse getting on. All the horses were ringy.

"Conroy was the one that put me to skinning dead cows the day I got there, just to see if I'd do what I was told. And the next day I started riding with him. I remember the first day out we saw six antelope, and I got excited and shouted that that was more antelope than I'd ever seen in my life. Conroy just grunted and said, 'When I was your age there'd be three hundred of them, just in there grazing with the damn cows,' and then he cussed and cussed. He was a bitter kind of man, but very good to me. The only thing he was ever scared of was electric storms like we sometimes had in the late winter. He would always get white and cross himself. He didn't talk much but he knew plenty and was very helpful to me.

"We were just riding and riding, looking after the stuff. We just rode all the time, in the snow, mostly, and way off you'd see some little specks and you'd ride to see if they were horses or cattle. If they were horses you didn't care, not in the winter, but if they were cattle we'd have to look them over and see if they were all right. You know the old saying that the eye of the master fatteneth the cattle? It's sure true. If you don't see them all the time, you aren't going to have any luck in the cattle business. You don't know whether a cow's got cut up on a fence or something or got worms eating on her and you don't know if she's able to get around and rustle. We'd find cows stuck in snowdrifts, too weak to get out. I remember one we pulled out one time. We hauled her out with our lariat ropes and then we'd shake the ropes off of her and she'd just fall down again. We tried head-and-tailing her, Conroy pulling on the horns and me on the tail, and every time she got up she'd say 'wawk' and charge old Conroy. The third time she knocked him off his horse into a snowbank. He gave her a kick, she was down again by that time, and he said, 'All right, die, damn you, die.' We'd take little calves up on the saddle with us and trail the old weak cows into the barn to be hay fed, and take the calves into the kitchen where the cook, she was a kindly woman, would give us some milk with warm water and sugar, and maybe a little whisky if the calf was bad off. You'd just let the milk run down between two fingers and the calf would go to sucking.

"They had Siberian wolfhounds there on the ranch. If we ran across wolf or coyote tracks, we'd take the hounds out with us and they'd run them down and kill them. The dogs used to sleep in the deep snow between the bunkhouse and the barn, out of the wind. Just tuck their nose under their tail and go to sleep. There was one old dog, she had a litter of puppies up in the barn loft. And I saw her, one day, dragging a whole antelope carcass up the stairs to the loft. I went up there and watched those puppies just tearing it apart and growling. That's how strong they were.

"Mostly we had grade Herefords on the Campstool, but one day we were riding and came across twelve old Frying Pan cows, with the Frying Pan brand, from down in Texas, just regular old longhorns, duns and brindles and smokies. I asked Conroy, 'How come those old mossy horns up here?' And he said they just kept them around out of sentiment for the old days, and that they were handy when they drove cattle for market or shipping. They'd let those old cows lead the herd right out and then they'd drive them back again or just let them graze back.

"The ranch was laid out up and down along the Union Pacific. Stations used to be close together—for the section crews. When there would be blizzards we'd stop in these stations to warm ourselves at those little round-bellied stoves. Of course we didn't get anything to eat at noon, but then we always ate a big breakfast, bacon and eggs and steak and hotcakes and lots of coffee. You couldn't make cigarettes while you were riding. Too much wind, and anyhow your hands would freeze, so I used to carry along a plug of tobacco. There was one week we rode it got down to forty below, and sometimes the wind would be fifty miles an hour. You'd wear all the clothes you had or could borrow. Long underwear, double-breasted wool shirts, pants out of corduroy or jeans, corduroy sheep-lined vests, two pairs of socks, then your boots and overshoes, a big sheep-lined ducking coat, a kerchief to pull over your mouth, leather cuffs to keep the wind from going up your sleeves, and mittens, although Conroy always wore a pair of silk gloves with buckskin gloves over them, just like the stage drivers did.

"One time Conroy took me out on the range and left me there to feed some cattle that couldn't move around after a big blizzard. I rode over to one of those little railroad stations so I'd have a sheltered place to sleep while I was out there. The trains weren't moving, but a snow plow had come through and had hit nine steers that were on the track and couldn't be seen for the flying snow. They weren't our cattle. They had a Broken Box brand, a very nice iron. They were all big steers and they were scattered up and down the track for a mile, some broken in the hind legs, some in the forelegs and some in both. They'd walked right over the right-of-way fences on the snowdrifts. I found the section foreman and told him he ought to kill those cattle. He had a six-shooter but was afraid to use it and besides he only had a few shells. I shot several of them. That was the only humane thing to do. When I ran out of shells I started hitting them in the head with a coal pick, and I was sick all the time I was doing it. There was one old steer that I'd shot and I'd hit in the head with the pick. He got up and started after me, holding that broken foreleg out like it was a club and he was going to beat me with it. I ran, or tried to run in all that heavy clothing and in the deep snow, and got behind a pole, and he just hit the pole behind me, wham, wham. I guess it's the only unpleasant memory I have of the Campstool Ranch, and I still have nightmares about it.

"It was cold but it was beautiful, and you could see so far. One day Conroy pointed out a little patch of white in the sky and asked me if I could see that little three-cornered cloud off there in the southwest. It was Pike's Peak and it was a flat 150 miles from there. The air was so clear. I always had good eyes and I didn't wear smoked glasses the way Conroy did to protect his eyes from the glare. One day we saw what we thought was a man, sitting on a cliff in that zero weather. Conroy said, 'If that's a sheepherder he's gone crazy and we'd better catch him before he hurts his self.' We rode up there and it wasn't a sheepherder but a bald eagle, the biggest one I'd ever seen or Conroy either. He flew away and a big pebble dropped out of his tail feathers as he took off and I've got it yet.

"The sheepherders had a lonely life and we looked down on them, although I don't know why we should. If we were riding the range and came to a sheep wagon, we always took advantage of it. Of course the herder would be gone in the middle of the day and we'd just make ourselves at home. Burn his firewood and eat his grub, baked beans or whatever he might have fixed, we not caring whether he ran short or not. Then we'd go on our way rejoicing.

"The herders lived in these little wagons, just a little home on wheels, with a bed and a number-eight stove, a little dropleaf table and a trunk to keep the things he needed, flour, bacon, beans, lard, coffee and firewood. There wasn't any timber in that country for firewood. Nights the herder would bring in his sheep and put them in a panel corral. It was a sad, lonely life, but we took no pity on them and always considered them lawful game. But there was one old man we never treated like that, because Conroy told me he had been a great bronc stomper in his day, one of the best, but alcohol was his downfall and after a while all he was fit for was sheepherding. You can imagine how terrible it must have been for him after an outstanding career as a horseman. He was allowed a couple of days off a month. Then the camp tender would bring another herder and bring the old man back to headquarters in the wagon, with a necktie on and his hair combed and his mustache all twisted up and his boots shined. Then he'd get in the hack and go to Cheyenne. Old Andy. What a wonderful old man, to be as old as he was. Like sixty. But they always had a hell of a time getting him out of Cheyenne. His parties never ended. He'd buy himself a lot of pure alcohol and shack up with a woman. And this one time they brought him back I'll never forget, he was bedraggled and his mustache was droopy and he had a faraway look in his eyes. They had to feed him and nourish him there at headquarters for a few days to get him back on his feet. Then they took him back out to his sheep wagon and his flock. We rode by his camp a day or so later and his sheep were just scattered all over hell. Some had been killed by wolves or coyotes and a lot had drifted over into other sheep camps. The sheep foreman went and found old Andy. He'd smuggled a couple of quarts of alcohol back from town with him. If it hadn't been getting on for spring, he'd have died. In the winter he would have. So they took him on his last ride into Cheyenne and I don't know what happened to him.

"Sometimes on Sundays we'd make a short day of it, and we'd ride broncs in the corral. They always kept a few around for the benefit of Eastern visitors, who always wanted to see some pitching horses. Or we'd lay around the bunkhouse and play harps and guitars and sing, or we'd have fights, usually in fun but sometimes not. There was a boy out there from Springfield, Missouri. His father was a railroad detective and had sent him a good Winchester with a box magazine, not that it had anything to do with what happened. There was another boy from Iowa, and one Sunday evening we got to joshing one another about the states we came from, and they came from all over. You know how fellows are about states. Like they never say 'Oklahoma fellow' but 'Oklahoma bastard.' And that you can always tell an Arkansawyer by the snot on his sleeve. They couldn't do much about me because they all thought I came from Arizona and that gave me quite a bit of prestige. They'd ask me about those center-fire California saddles with the girth in the middle and that was about all.

"Well, this boy from Missouri and the boy from Iowa was raw-hiding one another, and the Iowa boy says, 'They tell me Missourians ain't like anyone else. They tell me they got a shaft like a horse and it rattles when they trot.' Those two boys come together like a couple of buck deer and it was one of the bloodiest fights I ever saw. We all laughed at first but then we had to separate them before they killed each other. Then I played the French harp and after a while they shook hands and everything was all right.

"Old Conroy never talked much, but once in a while he'd tell me what a fine woman this lady cook was, there at the ranch. And I noticed him sometimes sitting up with her. I never kidded him about it; Conroy wasn't that kind of man. Then one day I had some time coming to me and was going into Cheyenne to have me a little party. And here come Conroy and the lady cook to ride in with me in the hack. She was all dressed up and somebody had given Conroy a shave and a haircut. He had on a celluloid collar and his boots were shined. The last I saw of them was in Cheyenne. They got married and never came back to the ranch. They bought a little café there in Cheyenne.

"This superintendent had sort of indicated I was next up after Conroy, to boss the cattle operation. This superintendent was a banker's son from back in Iowa or some damn place, and he'd been sent down there to learn the ranching business. He didn't know nothing about it, or how to get along with his men, either. He'd call you up on the carpet, you know, instead of coming out to the bunkhouse to talk to you. Just say, 'Will you please see me in my office.' It used to make old Conroy so damned mad, you know. 'Goddamn greenhorn,' he'd say, 'call a man on the carpet just like a goddamn railroad superintendent. Who does he think he is?' This fellow, this superintendent, used to ride a horse in a lope. Nobody but a damn Indian or a greenhorn does that in that country, in the snow. I'd seen somebody way off riding in a lope, and Conroy would say, 'Yeah, that's our boss. When he gets a little closer you can see that damn six-shooter banging up and down on his leg. He'll go somewhere with that some day and somebody will use the butt of it and lay his damn head open, just to see if there's anything inside.' Conroy didn't like him at all, and I guess that's one reason he left. But I thought he was a right agreeable sort of fellow, although a little silly. He wanted to be important, you know. He'd say, 'I was over on the south divide today and I saw some cattle; I don't know whether they were ours or somebody else's.' Well, what the hell difference did it make if you didn't know? The country was just plumb full of cattle; you saw them wherever you went.

"This superintendent had sort of told me that I'd be next in line after Conroy, but when the time came he picked a Norwegian fellow by the name of Pete Swanson. Pete was a good fellow and I liked him. He talked through his teeth like all those people from Scandinavia and other cold places. Pete was lazy and although he'd been there a long while he hadn't been riding the range as much as I had because he had one of those social afflictions that keeps you from riding horseback. Well, he started riding again, and he was a very fine horseman and a very good cowhand. He had a thin, fine Norwegian face, with a long, thin red nose and about a half inch of ginger-colored whiskers. He rode with a derby hat pulled down over his ears so it wouldn't blow off. And he rode standing up in short stirrups. Of course he had a reason for that, but then lots of us rode that way when we were riding in a high trot. But he always rode that way. I remember he and I rode thirty-five miles over into Colorado once in just three hours. That's pretty good riding.

"Pete was a good man, all right, but it kind of rankled in my mind that I hadn't got the job. It would have meant another five dollars a month, and I was making forty-five. Which was pretty good after Arizona and Texas. The superintendent put me in charge of the work on a little irrigation project they had—Pete didn't know anything about irrigation and I did, having worked in Arizona. But they had a sorry bunch of horses to work with so I just drew my time and headed back to Nebraska."

Chapter 14

KELLY had saved a little money and his mother sent him some more, urging him to buy some land of his own and settle down to ranching or farming if that was the life he wanted, but to settle down.

He met a convivial land agent for the Union Pacific and spent an evening with him in a saloon in Pine Bluffs, Wyoming, just across the line from Nebraska. The saloonkeeper, a man with a battered red face, said, "I don't allow nobody to come in here and get drunk without I get drunk with them," and proved it. He was, it developed, a formidable bronc rider and had an embossed and silver-mounted saddle back of the bar that he has won at the Cheyenne rodeo. The Cheyenne rodeo had also been the scene of his greatest humiliation. There was a bronc named Steamboat that few of the professional riders would even try to mount. The saloonkeeper bet that he could not only mount him but could stay aboard long enough to drink a bottle of beer. He climbed on the wild horse, stayed on and began drinking the bottle of beer that was handed to him. He might have won a substantial amount of money had he not, in a burst of cavalier spirit, decided to tip his hat to the ladies in the stands, and a split second later he landed headfirst on the ground, the beer bottle clenched in one hand, his hat in the other.

It was an exuberant evening, and at some point Kelly tied a pair of child's roller skates on his high-heeled boots and attempted to give a skating exhibition on the floor which was furrowed and pitted from horses' hoofs and random pistol shots. His fall, he was assured in good-natured fashion, was almost as spectacular as the one the saloonkeeper had taken off of Steamboat.

The next day he bought a half section of land at Kimball, Nebraska, for three dollars an acre, and the Union Pacific land agent congratulated him on his excellent judgment.

It was late to put in a crop and anyway he had no money left for seed or equipment. He stayed in a livery barn and went to work for the prosecuting attorney of Kimball County, a self-educated lawyer who slept in his office but owned a horse ranch and had only one eye, the result, it was said, of a nonlegalistic argument in a railroad section car. With the lawyer's son Joe, Kelly began rounding up mares and the spring crop of colts off the range and driving them into a four-section pasture. The spring rains had been heavy. The country was green and beautiful, the grass was rich and it was work that Kelly loved. He got his new saddle well broken in, and forever after that no matter how short he might be on other worldly goods he was never—except for one short, sad interval—without a saddle. He regarded it as a badge of his profession: horseman.

Each morning he and Joe would drive their horses, twenty-two of them, into a stock pen that bordered the railroad tracks. They would rotate horses on their daily rides, so that each horse was ridden only once in eleven days. They were, consequently, well rested, lively and frequently all but unmanageable, yet it took this kind of horse for the hard riding they were doing. The two young men would go into the pen, select their mounts, rope them and throw saddle and harness on. Hoboes from the jungle just down the railroad line would come and sit on the fence, cheering for the horses and looking, Kelly complained, like so many vultures waiting for one of them to be killed. They would mount the horses and ride them, bucking and pitching around the stock pen, letting them work off the surplus energy and get accustomed, once more, to the feel of a saddle and a man's weight. It was better to do these things on an empty stomach. After half an hour Kelly and Joe would dismount, go eat their breakfasts and then return to start the day's work on comparatively calm mounts.

They would ride through the country south of Lodge Pole Creek where the black-rooted buffalo grass and bluestem and sedge were thick and green. They would find the half-wild mares and their colts and drive or attempt to drive them in the direction of the trap, often riding five miles to make one of progress, always marveling at the speed of the spindly-legged little colts.

There were days of burning heat. There were electrical storms that would leave barbed wire fences charged with enough electricity to knock a man off his feet. There were days when the rain came in torrents and they rode standing in their stirrups to keep their seats dry—at the expense of getting their boots full of water; and storms when hailstones came as large as Ohio butternuts. They ranged west into Wyoming and south into Colorado, and Kelly had never had work so much to his liking.

Sometimes the lawyer himself rode with them. He would wear a black suit and congress boots, but he rode well, using long stirrups, roaring and shouting orders like a steamboat captain. He was noisy, gruff and impatient, but he liked Kelly and admired his horsemanship. He offered to put him in charge of a ranch he owned in Colorado. He would have nothing to do but care for horses. The other work, fence building, crop making, haying—everything would be done by others under Kelly's direction.

This was really what Kelly was looking for, but on the very day the offer was made he began, as he said, to "take curious." He had agonizing pains in his stomach, his head swam and when something was said to him it would seem that he had heard it all before, coming from a great distance. He had to dismount and ride back to Kimball in a wagon, not trusting himself to stay in the saddle. It was, he felt, time to go home and see his people. He might not be in this world for long.

On the range in both Wyoming and Nebraska he had led a healthy life. But on visits in Kimball he had developed the habit of drinking whisky and eating peanuts until he was sufficiently relaxed to collapse in bed in a hotel where a sign advised: "Guests will please remove spurs before retiring." On the day of his attack he had tried to fend off the results of a whisky-and-peanuts evening with a hearty breakfast of hot cakes, sirup, canned tomatoes and corrosively strong coffee.

He began working his way East. In Kearney, Nebraska, he worked in the alfalfa and cornfields until he was well enough physically to feel that he could afford an evening on the town. He had his picture made in a photographic studio, solemn-faced in his high-crowned Western hat, and he wandered through the streets. He avoided whisky and drank only beer with his salted peanuts. He spent the night in a hotel, rolling in agony and wondering if the hotel would ship his body back to his family if he died there, which seemed certain. For the first time in his career of wandering he was miserably lonely, not only disinterested in his surroundings but appalled by them.

Recovering, he moved on to Fremont, Nebraska, and worked in the grain fields until he had enough money to buy a railroad ticket East. He arrived in Elizabeth with his saddle, his boots and his Stetson hat, and moved into the house on Mary

Street, cool behind the elm-bordered lawn. The family doctor diagnosed his trouble as acute indigestion due to an unwise diet. In a few days he was working again in the shops of the Central Railroad of New Jersey, a long way from the sand hills and wide prairies and the rim rock and the half-wild mares. He often thought, then and later, that those months in Nebraska were the best springtime of his life.

Pay at the shops was good, better than anything he had known in the West, but the work still bored him. He was often sick, and when he was he would sit in his room with sheets of thick paper and a box of water colors trying to re-create the country and people and animals he had known so that he could show his family and friends: the mountains were sometimes pink or lavender or fiery red, the richness of the grassy plains and hills, the way the rain fell like curtains waving in a window, the rocky promontories, the figures of men and horses tiny under the wide sky, and the beautiful little colts running beside their mothers.

The Cheyenne saddle, sacked and tied with a lariat rope, hung in the attic, gathering mildew. The air was damp and soft and Kelly liked the smell of the Jersey meadows, but he remembered with greater pleasure the dry, tingling smell of the West.

He went to church with the family and frequently "walked out" with the girl from across the street, but his social life was limited. He did not feel at home with Quill's friends; they were younger and gayer. Kelly's companions, when he had any, were men from the shops. Drinking beer with them on Saturday nights in all the old familiar places, he often talked of where he had been and what he had done. They were friendly and warm, but they were only mildly interested. They were satisfied with life in the shops and did not understand the magic of the West that Kelly felt. The pull was stronger, now that he had been there, than it had ever been before.

Chapter 15

THE old Burlington coach rattled through the night, shut tight against the cold, the windows fogged with steam, the lights dimmed for the benefit of the snoring passengers, sprawled on the dust-smelling seats. Kelly and his brother rode facing one another. Quill slept, his head thrown back, his handsome features almost childlike in relaxation, his mouth slightly open. Kelly watched him with affection. Then, running his hand over the steamy window, he stared out into the night. Rain streaked across the glass, and while he watched it turned to snow. It was mid-April. When they left New Jersey the forsythia had been blooming and the jonquils budding. Here in Nebraska it was still winter.

The train stopped at dimly lighted, lonely stations—Ravenna and Hazard and Broken Bow. There was absolute darkness in between and beyond. Kelly compared the town names, seen dimly on the station platforms, with the map names he knew so well. Off to the left someplace would be the south branch of the Loup and beyond it the Platte. Someplace near them must be the middle branch of the Loup, and beyond it the vast reaches of Cherry County and Sheridan County and the Niobrara, the hills and dunes and the fertile valleys, all the land that was ready and waiting for settlers.

He wondered about Quill, whether it had been right to persuade him to return to Nebraska with him. While Quill adapted himself to anything in good humor and spirit, he was not enchanted with the West in the way that Kelly himself was enchanted. It meant no more to him that the Jersey shore or Manhattan Island; he liked all of them. Horses meant no more to him than trolley cars. Still, since his first trip West, Quill had been restless, and he needed no convincing. He was ready to go to Nebraska or Madagascar.

In his own mind Kelly had no doubt where he was going. He worked in the railroad shops only until his health returned and he had some money ahead. When

A Political Rally

More Good People

he bought a ring for the girl across the street the family thought perhaps he was, at last, settling down. But almost at the same time he bought a Colt six-shooter—and carefully noted the number, 8380, in the front of his diary, and a new Stetson hat. He tried to be sociable. He would go with men from the shops to the bars and the burlesque houses and the chop-suey joints and the clambakes. He went to church with the family and took the girl across the street to approved social affairs. But his heart wasn't in it. And he spent more and more time in his room, painting little pictures of things he remembered from the West. He framed them and gave them to members of the family for Christmas. And he was touched when his father took one of his paintings down to the shops to show the men, bragging on him. If his father was disappointed in Kelly's lack of interest in the shops, he did not show it. He listened carefully when Kelly explained to him the details of the Kinkaid Homesteading Act of 1904, asked intelligent questions about the land, the people, how crops were made and the stock raised. Kelly explained that he and Quill together could claim two sections of land, and with the half section he had bought the year before they would be on their way as farmers and stockmen.

They had crated their favorite books, a guitar and some French harps. They packed trunks of heavy clothing, including new overcoats their father bought for them. Kelly trussed up his saddle, the blanket in the fork, the stirrups tossed over, and the whole tied in a burlap sack, looking like a dressed turkey, and he convinced a dubious railroad agent that in the West a horseman's saddle always traveled as his personal baggage. Why, he said, this saddle had come all the way from Cheyenne that way.

And George Kelly had insisted on buying them a new plow, one that was said to be especially designed to cut through the thick, woolly sod of the plains. Kelly thought they might well have waited until they got settled to buy a plow, but now it was in the baggage car ahead with the crates and trunks and saddle. Kelly, his new Stetson riding squarely on his head, thought how well equipped and comfortable they would be compared with the days when they were beating through Arizona, New Mexico, Texas and all the rest. George Kelly had said that if they were coming West to stay they must do things properly, must go about it in businesslike fashion. He had given them extra money for the trip, for things they would surely need. It was money that might well have been used at home, where there were two younger children. But he did not want his sons traveling like hobos.

Kelly closed his eyes and thought of his father, a man of powerful brawny arms and the big, hard hands of a blacksmith, a sweet voice with which he liked to sing hymns to a stern but loving God, an elder in the church and in all things a man of great gentleness. The men in the shops admired and respected him and never called him anything but Mister Kelly; and George Kelly in his turn treated them with kindness and courtesy. It was understood that he could use his fists very well and had, in the remote past, done so, but only when kindness and understanding had been exhausted. He had none of his sons' impatience and restlessness. He went where the job took him, content wherever he was in a job well done, happy in the presence of his family in the center of a well-ordered world. And if he found it hard to share his sons' enthusiasm for new lands and new scenery, he always listened to their tales with the greatest interest.

"Alliance. . . . Alli-i-i-ance!" The conductor stood swaying in the aisle of the car, squinting at his silver watch in the dim light. Kelly rubbed his eyes and shook Quill awake, and they sleepily left the car. The cold struck them sharply in the face and the swirling snow stung their eyes. They stored their baggage, ate a heavy breakfast, went to the land office and to the Burlington colonization agent to talk about homesteads, and then to a livery barn. First they chose a horse for Quill, a placid, sturdy animal, for thirty-five dollars, and bought a used stock saddle to go with it. Kelly's eye, meanwhile, had been taken by a small horse that moved around the corral with spirit and nimbleness.

"He was long and low, a beautiful head and a fine crest. He carried his head up and he was well made for a small horse. He had irons all over him, including a Crow Indian brand, showing that he had changed hands many times and because of that his price was low. What he cost me was very modest for that much horse, forty dollars. The dealer caught him with a lariat rope and said he was pretty spooky, that he'd been running out all winter and spring. He asked if I didn't want him to top him off for me, and I said I'd do it. I put my hackamore on him and he struck at me with a forefoot, but I figured he'd get over that. I got the bridle on, then laid my Navajo and saddle up on top. I could tell he was getting ready to go, just full of beans, so I pulled the cinch pretty tight. That dealer says, 'You sure you don't want me to top him off?' and I said I guessed I could handle him. It made me kind of mad, although I hadn't been on a horse in a year. Just as soon as the weight of my left foot hit the stirrup that little devil dropped his head and I never saw a horse pitch and bawl so in my life. He hadn't been ridden in God knows when and he probably dumped the last man that rode him. He just hogged all over that corral, but finally I had him pulled up. I paid for him and rode him to the wagon yard.

"I called that horse Lovin' Henry. There was this singer, Ada Jones, that used to sing a song about her lovin' Henry Brown. That horse was anything but loving. But he was much horse and he gave me great pleasure and trouble, too. And embarrassment. Some time after that I was working in a livery barn in Kimball. I turned him out on the range with the owner's horses, so he was well rested and full of the devil. I brought him in one day and saddled him up. I wanted to ride him once in a while to keep him in shape and me, too, and besides I had to go to the courthouse on some business. Once I got in the saddle, he just threw himself all over the corral, pitching and squawling, then right on up through the middle of town and out to the other side of town where the courthouse was, just hitting the ground every once in a while and only long enough to go up in the air again. People all up and down the street stopped to watch and I was right proud of myself for the way I handled him. I really felt like the man on horseback. When I came out of the courthouse and went to the hitch rack I noticed the cinch was hanging a little loose, but I thought: Hell, he's had his romp out now, there's no use bothering. So I tied my McCarty on the saddle and picked up the reins. Just as soon as I swung my weight into the saddle that little devil dropped his head and bawled, and boy, howdy, how he pitched. He just got his head and his forefeet together, and I went over his head and the cinch came loose and there he went, right on back through the town, just hell-calarup, dragging the saddle by the McCarty. He ran between the barbershop and the drugstore, the saddle hitting bang! on one building and then bang! on the other, and then he headed west, right on out of town, dragging that forty-pound saddle after him at a full run. I had to pick myself up and dust off and walk back through town dragging my Navajo blanket, and all the people laughing and saying, 'What happened? Did you get throwed?' Of all the silly damn questions people can ask.

"Oh, he was much horse. One time after I'd ridden him fifty miles in a day I thought I'd see if he had any fight left in him. Fifty miles in the sand hills is a big day's ride for anybody, man or horse. I reached around and put my hand on his loins and he started right in with me, just like he had that morning when I first took him out of the corral at the wagon yard. Old Lovin' Henry. Not really a good horse at all, but the kind a young fellow will buy just for the excitement."

Chapter 16

ALLIANCE boiled with boom-town business. Saloons and dance halls operated around the clock. Each Burlington train brought in more Kinkaiders, and still more came overland in wagons; plows and cookstoves, washtubs and crates of chickens with them. There were the adventurous young men, costumed according to bizarre Eastern notions of how Westerners dressed. There were still-hopeful middle-aged men with their weary families; and there were almost desperate old men, looking for what was probably their last chance. They filled the hotels and wagon yards and camped on the outskirts of town. They thronged the land office and clustered around the Burlington's colonization agent. They asked earnest questions and went on long, hard trips through the raw country with "locaters," men who had come to the western Nebraska country long enough before to know it well. For a fee they would help a newcomer find a promising piece of land on which to file a claim. For the most part the locaters had been homesteaders themselves and were glad to see settlers come. If circumstances dictated, they might reduce or forego the fee. The sooner they could get the country "settled up," the sooner they would have the schools and roads and post offices they wanted. And each new homesteader was an ally in their struggles with the cattlemen and powerful cattle companies. The cattle interests had fought the homesteaders or Kinkaiders, sometimes with guns, sometimes with intimidation, but more often with bogus claims. A cattleman would file claims on adjoining sections of land in the names of ranch hands and relatives, pay the claim fee, and build a tiny shack and plow up a few acres of ground to meet the minimum requirements of habitation and cultivation. Recently, however, the federal government had stepped in and prosecuted some of the cattlemen for the fraudulent claims, and the outlook for the Kinkaiders was brighter.

The Kelly brothers struck east from Alliance, the elder on the wild, hard-mouthed little pony ironically named Lovin' Henry, the younger on a gentle, plodding horse more suited to his inexperience. They headed north into the vastness of Cherry County. They rode through a blizzard, brief and furious, and through torrents of rain. They avoided the occasional large ranches and stayed, when they could, with homesteaders. They spent one night on an abandoned farm, sleeping in a pile of prairie hay left in the sod-built barn of a settler who had either become disheartened or disillusioned in the stark country. They breakfasted on raw eggs provided by a castaway hen, and rode to the farm of a man named Jack Gannow.

Gannow and his wife made them welcome and hoped they would settle near them. The next day Gannow rode out with them to show them two adjoining sections of land in Survey Valley, which, he thought, might be just what they wanted. A railroad survey had been made there once. The two sections were divided by a creek. The bottom land on either side was black and rich, and the uplands promised good haying. There would be no shortage of water; a sand point driven into the loose soil would soon tap a plentiful supply. There were two dummy claims already on the land, put up by a cattle company, but they would not stand up in court. Two shacks had been built, neither large enough for a man to stretch his length. And a little grove of cedars and cottonwoods had been planted around each of the shacks as a token of cultivation.

Gannow rode away and left them to ponder. Kelly and his brother rode over the land, stopping to scratch at the soil, studying the way the slopes were drained. Kelly recalled that a friend in Kimball had offered him his choice of any twelve horses in his stable in exchange for his equity in land he had bought from the Union Pacific. With that as a start they could have a horse ranch. There was plenty of pasture, plenty of crop land for feed and other necessities, plenty of water. They could break and train and sell horses. They could get a few grade cows, sell their first calf crop, get a good bull, build up a little herd. Break up and plow just enough of the land to raise feed and supply the kitchen. Get a milk cow, keep some chickens. . . . Kelly often recalled it with regret.

"We rode over those two sections, just looking and looking. Then we got off our horses and sat on the ground and looked some more. And we got to thinking. We would have to ride up to Merriman or Chadron to file our claims. About sixty miles we'd have to ride. And we got to studying how far this land was from a railroad, and from any town with lights and people. We couldn't make up our minds if we wanted to live way off from civilization that way. Besides we already had this other land I'd bought, down there by Kimball. Finally Quill said why didn't we just flip a coin, heads we go and tails we stay. It came up heads, so we got on our horses and rode back to Jake Gannow's to tell him thanks and farewell.

"Now there's where opportunity really knocked on my door with a big dollar in her hand and I turned the other way. Ain't that a hell of a way to do? I'd probably be a rich man today, and if I painted pictures at all it would just be for pleasure and not for money. That's the way a boy brushes it off. I don't regret anything I ever did, but it's what I didn't do. Like that. There in Survey Valley. But your life is laid out for you, anyhow. You're going to have a good time and meet some fine people no matter how you go, if you live in a seemly manner and stay out of the damn jails."

The two brothers rode south again where the land was more closely settled, looking for land. But where people were already settled the price of land per acre was far too high. They heard of the Antelope Flats and the name intrigued them, so they rode to Oshkosh on the South Platte.

"It was one of the most beautiful countries I ever saw, there at Oshkosh. Settlers were peddling their relinquishments and peddling them high. Oshkosh was a very small town but a prosperous one with a store, a hotel, a wagon yard, a couple of saloons and lots and lots of gamblers. Some of them kept fighting chickens and some kept race horses and they would bet on anything, on how fast a boy could run to the corner or how far an old man could spit. It was one of the sportiest little towns I ever saw. We kept our horses at a wagon yard run by a fellow who supplied horses for the stage that brought mail and passengers from Sidney. He liked to gamble, too—there was always a game going—and I got a job tending horses for him. He had a wrangler that brought fresh horses in from the ranch, but I cared for them there at the yard. The wrangler, a big, black-headed fellow, when he got in with the horses would kick off his boots and lay down on a cot in the office, drink a half-pint of whisky and go to sleep with a fresh cigarette in his mouth. He would snore and the cigarette would burn right down till it got into that thick black mustache and then it would sizzle and go out. You'd think the smell would wake him up, but then horse wranglers aren't much bothered with smells.

"A gambler had disappeared the year before and he'd left a big, brown thorough-bred horse there at the wagon yard along with one of the biggest, finest jackasses I ever saw. The horse had been there so long his feet had grown long—he still had on his racing plates—and I never took him out of his stall. He was a killer. They had always carried water to this jackass, too. Just kept him on a halter. But I thought: Hell, I know all about jackasses, I'll just lead him out to the trough instead of carrying water in for him.

"In the corral at the yard was a big bunch of horses, mostly geldings, you know. When I led that jack out he was so joyful to be out in the open he just tore out with me at the end of the halter, just tore out for those geldings as fast as he could go, a-braying all the way. I tried to hold on but I stepped on a corncob and went down. And you never saw such a scared bunch of horses in your life. He mounted them and he brayed and he chewed around on them, liked to scared those old eunuchs to death. He was just having a good time, but those geldings were trying to crawl through the fence and kicking it the hell to pieces. Some loafers from the street heard the commotion and saw the horses coming through the fence and they ran in and helped me catch the horses that had got through the fence. I left there right after that.

"Old Quill had been working in a café. He liked the town, being a pretty good gambler himself and liking the excitement. There was also a prize fighter named Cardwell in that town, amongst all the other sporting articles. Now Quill was a good-sized boy and strong, too, and the gamblers there in the café got to egging him on and betting him he couldn't stay three rounds with Cardwell. Quill put up his money and Cardwell flattened him in the second round. The gamblers all complimented him on what a good fight he had put up, which was pretty nice because I think a few of them had bet on Quill, and they had lost their money, too. We took off right after that."

Lewellen, Ogallala, Big Springs, Julesburg, Chappell, Lodgepole, Sidney—the two brothers rode on and on, their quest becoming more and more indefinite. In Kimball, where a year before he had been rounding up mares and colts, Kelly went to work in a livery barn and sent for the trunks and gear they had left in storage. With what money he had left he bought a brightly painted little wagon, the only new wagon he was ever to own. He and Quill loaded their belongings in the wagon and took off once more, this time for Perkins County, where, they heard, there was better crop land, better watered and richer than the land around Kimball. They camped out along the way, first along Lodgepole Creek and then the South Platte, enjoying themselves. The Perkins County land was good, just as they had heard, but they were out of money and did not feel they could ask their father for more. They plowed sod land and harrowed corn for a farmer near Grant, finishing on July third, earning eleven dollars between them.

"I rode Lovin' Henry into town on the Fourth of July, and he pitched all the way like he usually did the first thing in a day's riding. Some people saw me and said, 'Will you ride that little horse up here this afternoon for our Fourth of July celebration? We'll make you up a little pot.' I said it didn't make me no never mind. So Quill and I went up there that afternoon, leading Lovin' Henry. The town was full of people, and there were flags flying and kids shooting off firecrackers and I figured Lovin' Henry would give me the ride of my life. We got to this little field where the crowd was. No corral, no fences or anything. I climbed on Lovin' Henry and slapped him with my hat and did every damn thing but for once in his life that little sonofagun wouldn't do nothing. Just stood there. Well, then they brought up a big brown horse that was supposed to be pretty wild and asked if I was afraid to ride him. I said no, and climbed on. But that horse just pitched a couple of pitches. The crowd was all around him, yipping and yowping, and a drunk fellow was standing in front of us yelling, and I guess the horse was just plumb scared. I don't know as I blame him. So I got down and collected the pot, which was six dollars and a half, and stuck it in my pocket. People started complaining that I hadn't put on a show, and old Quill stood up and let them have it. You needn't be afraid of a whole damn town full of people if Quill was behind you. Then they brought up another horse, a sorrel, wanting me to ride him. I guess I would have, but a fellow about my age came up and whispered to me, 'Don't have anything to do with that damn horse. If he can't throw you, he'll rare over backward and fall on you and try to kill you.'

"So I told the people I reckoned I had earned my money. And while they were yow-yowing around and old Quill standing there cussing them, this other fellow comes up. He was the town barber, and he had curly hair and a pink and white skin and a derby hat and a shiny rubber collar with an already-tied bow tie. He was very drunk and he said, 'By God, I'll ride him.' And before anyone could say anything he had one foot in the stirrup and was trying to get up when that horse just busted him, throwing him about ten feet. He got up and looked around and dusted himself off and said, 'I could ride him if I could only get on him.' And he says to me, 'Will you hold him for me?' So I got hold of that damn horse's ears and pulled his head down to my chest. Well, the barber got on and shouted, 'Let the sonofabitch go!'

76

I never saw a man go as high or come down as hard as that fellow did. Right on that derby hat. Just drove it right down over his ears. The people didn't yell any more. They'd had their fun. Six dollars and a half worth.

"The fellow that warned me about the horse came up and we got acquainted. His name was Claude Carter. They had a little ranch out from town and suggested we come out there and help with the prairie hay, so we did. His brother Riley was there, home from veterinary college in Kansas City, and their father, too. They were raising horses, general purpose horses, and they all came from Missouri. We unpacked our trunks and hung our overcoats to sun and air, and the grasshoppers just ate them up. Those big old yellow grasshoppers.

"Quill did the cooking, Riley studied his veterinary books and Claude and I cut prairie hay. He had a mower with a buncher on it, and we'd just drive out and cut this free grass. Every little way you'd trip the buncher and it would leave a little bunch of that good prairie hay. Then we'd come along in the afternoon with a barge on the wagon and take it into town and sell it for seven dollars and a half a load, sell it to the livery barn and doctors and people like that who kept horses. It was pretty doggone nice.

"Nights we would sit around and talk. The Carters, being from Missouri, used to talk a lot about the Ozarks, what a beautiful country that was, how well timbered it was and how the water was plentiful. It all sounded pretty nice. Quill never did care much for that Nebraska country, so we decided we'd go down to the Ozarks and look around. I wrote to Lott the Land Man in Kansas City, and I sold my equity in the land at Kimball, and we took off again. For the Ozarks.

"I'd sort of got Nebraska out of my system. The only way to have made it there was to get land that was way to hell and gone off from people and everything. We were just young fellows and restless and we liked people. I still do."

Chapter 17

IN his late years Kelly could remember, in the finest detail, the days of his youth, the names and faces, the places and the mellowness of the earth he had plowed, the taste of smoked sausage, the fragrance of wild flowers crushed under his feet, the excitement of a new land beyond the hills, the waving stands of prairie grass shining with dew in the morning. But while these things came back with startling clarity, the middle years of his life were a confused jumble.

Part of this was the mental presbyopia of age: the events of many years ago emerge more clearly than the facts and sensations of last month or last year. But in Kelly's case there was much that he did not care to remember. It wasn't that he had anything of which to be ashamed. It was just that he was, by all the measurements he had been taught, a failure.

He was never idle, although his friends sometimes confused the faraway look in his eyes with laziness. Good-natured and hard-working, he was, nevertheless, always restless, impatient, curious, and for many years he drifted from one menial task to another. Even as a child he had been eager to throw off childishness and do a man's work. His hands were those of an honest working man, broken, calloused, strong and willing. They had felled trees and cut them into boards, had built houses and coffins, fences and wagons; they had shaped iron to horse's hoofs, sharpened plowshares and guided them through tough, virgin soil. They had, more often than not, worked for other men and had kept little of what they made. Yet they had never been raised in anger against the men who grew rich from his labor or profited by his improvidence. He had a high regard for the Golden Rule and kept it in an almost constant state of imbalance, doing more for others than he either expected or wanted others to do for him.

All his life he suffered from a kind of economic disorientation. He usually did the right thing but at the wrong time, place and price. He was an intimate of the earth and the things that grow in the earth, but he never managed land and crops in a way that would make him rich and respected as a man of property. He loved farm animals, but his love bore little or no relation to the current market price for stock; he often went without food himself to feed stock that would, in that day's market, not bring the price of the food.

Foresight and clever dealing were beyond him, and he was only vaguely aware of it when he was the victim of sharp practice. Time and again he met opportunities that, firmly grasped, might have made him the substantial sort of person his people had been. He would accumulate material goods only to forsake them because they were a hindrance to what he wanted to do next. He was, he admitted, "too quick to take a notion and too quick to get charmed up." When this happened there was nothing to do but go. He was conscious of his improvidence and was not proud of it, as a truly reckless soul might be, but there was little he could do about it. That was the way he was.

He came to the Missouri Ozarks from Nebraska, a little money in his pocket from the sale of his bright new wagon and his team of horses and the tools with which he had planned to become a Nebraska homesteader. They had been sold at distress prices. Having decided that the unseen Ozarks were the place for him, he was of no mind to hang around and wait for a good offer.

He was delighted with the new country. The natives called it wood-and-water country. "We don't have much," they would say, "we got a poor land. But, thank God, we got wood and water." A man who had been on the bare, dry plains as Kelly had knew what they meant, and he liked it. And with what little cash he had he made a down payment on an abandoned two-hundred-acre farm in Polk County, Missouri. The old house had burned at the time of the Civil War and there was no shelter, but it was, in the fall of the year, a pleasant place to camp. A clear stream wandered through the land, tumbling from rocky ledge to sandy basin. The pleasant clearings were bordered with oaks, and back in the woods the maples were like crimson bonfires. He visited with the men and boys who came through the woods hunting squirrels and with the women who came to wash their laundry in the stream, spreading it on the sun-warmed rocks to dry. He rode with the men at night, hunting possums, raccoons and foxes in the hills, learning to read clearly the bugle notes of the hounds. He visited with families for miles around, went with them to their "meetings," learned to sing their fundamentalist hymns and marveled at their sweet singing voices and the fervor of their lamentations. He went to their box suppers and ice-cream socials and thought they were as fine a people as he had ever known. They were friendly and unhurried and good-humored, unlike the grimly eager, land-hungry settlers in Nebraska.

"They were very kind and good to me, and I liked both Polk County and the people. It was very interesting to live among hill people for a change, both there and, later on, over in Arkansas. But I never could understand some of the strange things they did and said and believed. Like pulling out a cow's tongue and scraping it and rubbing in salt and pepper to cure the holler-horn. Or scarifying the roof of a horse's mouth for the lampas. Or putting a rock in the cookstove oven to keep hawks away from the house.

"A book peddler had been through that country peddling copies of *The White Slavers, or Sold into Shame* or some damn fool book like that. And all the girls and womenfolk were quite spooky about it and distrustful of newcomers, thinking they might be white slavers. They finally accepted me, all right, but still they were all quite gullible.

"I remember one time there was an old soldiers' reunion in Bolivar. About five or six whole generations of one family from back in the hills had come into town for the festivities. They just parked themselves on the stoop of the hotel to eat their lunch, and they were just making a hell of a mess there with chicken bones, apple cores, melon rinds, peanut shells, tobacco juice and one damn thing and another. The hotel manager came out, saw what was happening and didn't do anything but pull out his watch, look at it and say, 'Folks, in just five minutes they're going to have the free balloon ascension out on the edge of town.' They all just lit right out of there to look for that balloon. That's the way they were, and I liked them.

"But I wasn't getting much of anywhere there in Polk County. I had got back a little of the money I'd put into that half-section of land in Nebraska, and I put that into this Polk County land, clearing and fencing it. But that land was just plumb worn out and I didn't have sense enough to know it. In those old days farmers used to brag about how many farms they had worn out. Those old boys used to say, 'Why, son, by the time I was your age I had wore out three farms.' Well, this one was worn out, so I rented some other land to try to make a crop, and I worked at one thing and another for other people. And I got to doing some horse trading, which was one of the local industries.

"There was this horse trader there in Polk County, a likable fellow and a smart one. We got to be quite good friends and did a lot of trading. He said to friends of mine—and they told me about it afterward—he said, 'Kelly sure has got a lot of sense about horses, can read their teeth and all and is about as good a judge of a horse as I know. But he sure is a sorry horse trader.'

"Where he said I was a sorry horse trader, he meant anything in the way of a horse I saw that I liked, I wanted it. I was willing to pay for it and I didn't want anything that was just nearly as good or easier to trade for. If I took a liking for it I would give boot to get it, instead of taking boot. And taking boot is the only way you get ahead in horse trading. If you always give boot, you'll get skinned.

"That fellow was about horse trading the way a gambler is about gambling. Anyway he could beat you, he'd do it, and often did. He gave me a good trimming, all right, but I didn't hold it against him because that's the way horse trading is.

"But the real trimming I got was down in Howell County, Missouri. That's where the horse traders of the world came from. That was when I was on my way to Arkansas.

"Everyone was talking about that rich land over there in Arkansas around Newport and Oil Trough and in there, that rich cotton land, and I decided Arkansas was the place for me. I just let my land there in Polk County go. I just wrote the fellow that I didn't want it, and gave up what I'd paid into it.

"I hauled a load of grain as far as Springfield which gave me a little running money, and then struck off east and south on the Old Rock Bridge-Memphis road, through Mansfield, Mountain Grove, Cabool and Willow Springs, down that way. It lies right along the crest of the Ozarks and is very beautiful, but you were in a hell of a mess if you got off the road.

"I had a good gelding in my team and a mare that seemed pretty good when I traded for her in Polk County, but she began to fall off on me and I thought I'd better trade when I could.

"Somewhere down there in Howell County, maybe around Willow Springs, I camped on a creek and right after I set up my camp some horse traders came in, several wagons with a whole string of animals. I walked over after they'd set up their camp and looked over their stuff. They didn't have any horse stock that I'd trade for. It was worse than that ailing mare of mine. But they showed me a good-looking old smooth-mouth mule. When I went to look at him he just snorted and pulled back and seemed to have plenty of zip. I traded for him.

"The next morning when I got up the horse traders had all left. I harnessed up the mule and he started out just fine, working with the gelding. But after about a mile he started slowing down and I had to begin tapping him with the whip. All I had was a buggy whip; I never needed anything to beat a horse with, so I just carried a light buggy whip. I tapped him again and again, and he just kept on inching along, dragging back until the singletree was rubbing the wagon wheel, just really taking out on me. And the horse was getting more nervous all the time, what with me tapping the mule and him having to haul the mule as well as the wagon.

"I stopped and got to studying the mule. He was old and sick, and those traders had high-lifed that old mule, fed him whisky or some damn thing. I could smell something on his breath. They had given him enough to keep him going until they got away from there. The mare I traded was poorly, but this old mule, once he sobered up, was just a deadhead. I could hardly lead him.

"I had a little mare that I had been leading because she was a fine buggy animal and I hadn't wanted to use her hauling a wagon. But I had to put her in harness to help lead that old mule. I dragged that old bastard till his head got sore from the halter, and it was a strain on the horses, too.

"I went on down into Arkansas through Mammoth Springs and down Black River, in through there, and it was just wonderful country, almost tropical, with the big black gum trees and the sweet gums and the cypresses, all very beautiful. Someplace down in there I traded that old mule to a Negro fellow. I told him the mule was no good, but that maybe he could use him in trading for something else. He gave me five dollars for him. Five dollars and an old guitar.

"I got to Newport, and it was a wonderful old river town, all new and strange to me and quite appealing, just everything in the world there to entertain people. They made a lot of pearl buttons there from mussels fished out of the White River. One part of the town was called Button Cutters Row, and you could always smell the stink of the mussel meat they threw away. It was a hard-drinking, hell-raising town, and they used to say their three principal products were buttons, booze and babies. They were tough, but everyone had a good time. I camped outside the town and went in. I saw a minstrel show called *The Sweetest Girl in Dixie*, which was nice, and I spent one night at a little hotel, which was very pleasant after camping on the road. And I ate at a restaurant where they served every damn thing. Squirrel dumplings, which I didn't care much for, and possum with sweet potatoes, which was very good, and roast coon with dressing, which was just delicious. Those fellows in town, there, they'd get to drinking and the best thing they could think of to eat was roast coon with dressing. None of these hamburgers and things that people eat nowadays. And there were street peddlers. An old Negro man had a little steam wagon, and I can still hear the cry he had. He'd cry:

"'Hah-ah-ah-t weenies' in a very high-pitched voice, and then:

"'Co-o-o-ld chicken' in a very deep voice, and then:

"'If y'all don't believe it,

"'Come put yo' finger on de weenies,

"'Lay yo' han' on de chicken,

"'Hah-ah-ah-t weenies, an'

"'Co-o-o-ld chicken!'

"Hot weenies and cold fried chicken, you know, and both very good, and his voice was very musical.

"I rented some land there, out toward Oil Trough Bottom. It's very fertile land, almost all planted to cotton. The cotton land runs right up to the road and there were old-time log houses set up on cypress blocks with brick chimneys. In the old, old days they used to ship bear fat out of Oil Trough. In those days there were lots of brown bears and they killed them for the oil that could be made from the fat. They used it for cooking and hair oil and every damn thing, and it was supposed to be very fine. They'd hollow out logs and fill them with this oil and then raft them down the river to New Orleans. They called those logs 'oil troughs.' The bears were all gone when I got there.

"I rented land from a big plantation and I hauled cotton for them to make a little money and hauled timber, hickory stock and stuff like that, for the plantation sawmill. I'd use plantation mules because the work was too heavy for my team, and I'd haul maybe three bales of cotton into Newport through that loblolly mud, and I'd buy plantation supplies for them. I might take a drink, Yellowstone whisky, mostly, but not much more than that, although that was a town where everyone used to just go wild with drinking. Still I had to manage that wagon and team on those little ferryboats to get across the river, and you couldn't do that if you'd been drinking. The ferry would carry three wagons at a time and you had to watch your step.

"The water got up on my rent land and stayed for two weeks so I didn't make a cotton crop, and I moved off of the plantation and rented another little place. I farmed a little, made a little crop of sweet potatoes and cotton, but mostly I hauled timber. That's very nice, you know. When it was too wet to farm you could always haul timber."

Chapter 18

ALTHOUGH it was the land's cotton richness that had drawn Kelly to Arkansas, he found that cotton had little appeal for him. Stoop labor wasn't meant for a horseman. But a good teamster had a place in the woods. Arkansas was cutting more timber than ever before. In the river bottoms and the hills portable sawmills were set up everywhere. Horses and teamsters were needed to haul logs from the woods to the mills, to the yards and railway sidings.

Kelly found that he liked such work. He traded for logging horses of his own, and learned to skid the big logs onto a wagon to take to the mills for slabs and staves, spokes and furniture stock; to use a mud boat and a lizard and to handle the great log wagons with their eight wheels boxed to keep the gummy mud from hanging in the spokes; to judge the number of board feet a log of white oak, gum or cypress would make when cut.

When Kelly wasn't working in the woods with his own team he often watched a giant Negro ox-driver named Ab Green handling draft cattle, sometimes as many as six yoke at a time. Ab was six and one half feet tall, had arms like stovepipes and a deep rich voice that, Kelly thought, sounded like the bass notes of an organ played softly in the temple of the woods. Ab's bull whip was so long and heavy that no one else could swing it. Yet Ab handled it as lightly as Kelly would handle a buggy whip, floating it out and making it crack like a pistol shot at the side of the animal whose name he called, never touching them. With the lash of his whip he could break the backs of rattlesnakes that came down out of the hills into the cool, swampy timberland in the heat of the Arkansas summer. He showed Kelly how the cattle were taught to respond to their names and to obey commands, how to swing and crack the whip without touching them or cutting them up, how to plait a popper out of sea grass. They became close friends although Ab never called him anything but Mister Kelly, with

Fourth of July Races

Coffee at the Wagon

the deference a Southern black man was supposed to use in addressing a white. Yet, he confided, he had named all his cattle for various prominent white citizens. So, when Ab stood on the balls of his feet, swung the mighty whip and softly called out, "Yo', Joe, now!" it was a wry tribute to a landowner named Joe Epps; and when he smoked up a steer called Dave he was really talking about Dr. David Bateman, whom Ab had never called anything but Mister Doctor in person.

Much later in Arkansas when Kelly was without a team of his own and needing work he became a bullwhacker himself. He was in the hill country of Arkansas and told a sawmill operator he had learned to handle oxen in the swamps, where the real bull-whackers lived. He didn't admit that he'd never actually driven, but had only watched the masterful Ab Green.

"We went out to his place and found the steers. The leaders were named Duke and Dard, and the wheelers were Red and Tap. They'd been on grass and hadn't worked in a long time and were really feeling top-hole. I found out which side they worked, which was near side and which was off side. With an ox team you walk on the near side, you know, on the left.

"I'd fixed myself up with a whip. I got the bows and got old Duke and put him up, put the bow through the yoke and keyed it in. Then I called Dard, and he marched right around and I put his bow and key on. I talked to them like I'd known them always. I got the snap chain and put the big hook in the ring of the yoke. Then I got Red and Tap and yoked them and took them to the wagon.

"That was a big, heavy wagon, a Studebaker, and it had one of those tail brakes, set between the bolster and the axle and worked crossways with a ratchet and a long bar. Then we started down this long hill toward the sawmill, on the banks of the river. I walked along, talking to them, and everything was going very nicely. But then the wagon got to moving faster than I could walk, and I jumped on the wagon and set the brake. I wasn't used to a tail brake like that. The hill got steeper and the wagon got to rolling faster, and then the damn brake jumped off. I should have fastened it in place with a chain, but I hadn't. I jumped off and tried to fix it but couldn't, and the cattle got to trotting and then got to running and we were coming down the hill just hell-calarup. You know an ox or a cow either one, when they're running and you see them from behind, are about as comical as anything in the world. They weren't made to run, but these animals couldn't do anything but run with that heavy wagon pushing them. When we got to the sawmill we were just going like hell, and the men at the sawmill were standing around and laughing and yelling, 'Sook, sook, sook, suck, suck, suck,' and I was just plumb scared. That road ended right at the river's edge where there was a little bluff. There was supposed to be a ferry there and it might have stopped us, but it wasn't there. We were sure headed for disaster, because that log wagon was so heavy it would have sunk all four of those cattle. But God was sure with me. Just before we got to the riverbank the key came out of the off-wheeler's bow and the yoke came down and crammed him up against the wagon and stopped the whole damn parade. It didn't hurt him much and it sure saved all the rest of us.

"I drove cattle there all that summer. There's few things in my life that I've got to be proud of. But that's one accomplishment that's always given me a lot of satisfaction, although I guess it wouldn't to anybody but me. That's being an ox-driver. There was always a certain prestige in being able to drive cattle to a wagon, and there just aren't many bullwhackers any more."

He lived on a succession of small, rented farms, and when he was not working as a teamster he put in a few crops, cotton, corn, turnips, sweet potatoes. His house was usually an old log cabin or a tiny frame shack. He bathed in the rivers and streams. He traded his six-shooter for a Winchester rifle and hunted squirrels, possums and coons for food, never for the pleasure of killing. He caught bream and catfish for neighborhood fish fries where the choctaw beer was plentiful. He went to parties and learned to plunk out country dance tunes on the guitar he had received in trade for the dead-head mule. He did not, however, like the mournful folk songs the hill people sang and cared nothing for the dreary fates of Lord Rindel and Barbry Ellen. He liked the gay music of minstrel shows and never missed one if he could help it. When he could afford it he would spend a roistering Saturday night in town.

He had frequent attacks of malaria, as did anyone who lived in the swamps and river bottoms, and he doctored himself with quantities of store-bought patent medicines without effect. He tried all the home remedies—a teaspoonful of red pepper washed down with a pint of hot cider, herb teas made from elderberry root, blade fodder, rattlesnake weed, peach bark, sheep manure and the juice of possum grapes. He drank toddies of grain alcohol mixed with hot water and sugar to stop the chills, and he rubbed his aching body with Lightning Oil and Orang Utan Liniment. None of it seemed to help. His only hope was to move out of the swampy country.

He sold his team, his farming and timber tools, all at a sacrifice. He sold what crops he had in the ground, unharvested, paid his debts, and started north and east, taking with him a crate of books and the Cheyenne saddle, carefully wrapped and sacked. These were his total possessions—much less than he had had four years earlier when he and Quill had set out for Nebraska to find homesteads and fortunes.

He returned to Missouri, looking around for a share-cropping arrangement, and, finding none, moved across the Middle West, often guided by nothing more than the location of a state or county fair. He admired the rich displays of fruit, grain and vegetables, the prize horses, cattle and swine, envying the solid farmers who stayed in one place and raised these things. Finally he reached Bucyrus, the town that in his childhood had always meant security and permanence. His grandfather was dead, his grandmother an invalid. His grandfather's wonderful house now belonged to someone else; the fine red bricks were painted an ugly dun color. The town itself was larger, busier, less personal. Only the fine, level farmland was unchanged.

He wanted to go on to Elizabeth, but he did not want to get there broke. He got work in a blacksmith shop whose owner, years before, had been a hammer boy for his father. He joined Company A of the Eighth Infantry Regiment of the National Guard, went to pigeon roasts and oyster fries, sang "Put on Your Old Grey Bonnet" and "Has Anybody Here Seen Kelly?" He had a severe recurrence of malaria, lost his old job and got a new one as a railroad freight handler. He saved some money, living frugally at a railroad hotel, bought a new suit of clothes and in the spring got a job taking a trainload of export cattle to New York. He persuaded the conductor to let him ride in the lookout of the caboose.

"That was how I got to really see and appreciate the Horseshoe Curve. I'd been around it time and again when I was a boy, but this time I really saw it, from the lookout of the caboose. And Lancaster County. My father had always told me how beautiful Lancaster County was, that was where he was born. And I always thought it was just because he was an old man and it was his home. But when I saw it that time I saw what he meant, Lancaster County in the spring of the year. I don't believe there's any more beautiful country. And that wonderful bridge across the Susquehanna River." He delivered his trainload of cattle in Jersey City, changed into his new store suit, got a haircut and a shave and went home for the first time in four years.

Chapter 19

HE did not want to go back in the shops, Kelly told his father. He just wasn't made for the shops. George Kelly said there was a job as night hostler in the roundhouse of the railroad yards, but Kelly said he'd rather work in the open, and preferably in the daylight. His father, whatever his feelings may have been about Kelly's waywardness, said there was good farming country up around Somerville, that perhaps he might invest in a little farm there for Kelly to manage. Kelly was cheered and went off into the country to look at farm land. He visited a model farm owned by Senator Joseph Frelinghuysen and was taken on as a general handyman. He was happier with his work than he had been in a long time. The pay was good, the quarters and board were excellent and the farm had the best of everything in stock and equipment.

The superintendent was a graduate of an agricultural college and asked him his preference in jobs. Kelly said that by inclination he was a teamster but that he could do anything. The farm had one team of horses that had been runaways and were due to be shipped out for sale. Kelly took them, gentled them and made dependable work horses of them. He sat up nights with a valuable Clydesdale mare that was about to foal her first colt. Within a month he was made boss of the horse barn, was given a substantial raise and was very pleased with both the job and himself. Weekends he would take the train to Elizabeth with a jar of sweet cream and a basket of fresh fruit for the family. He seemed on his way to becoming a staid and sober citizen. It was one of the many times in Kelly's career when he might, merely by staying in one place, have achieved the sort of success and respectability everyone in his family wished for him.

But in the fall he went to Waterbury, Connecticut, where his brother Quill was working for a brass company. Quill had married the girl from across the street with whom Kelly had "walked out" years before. They had two little daughters, and the reunion was a happy one for all of them. They had so much fun together that Kelly stayed on with them, forgetting the good job on the Raritan Valley farm, and getting, instead, a job as a freight wagon driver for the brass company. He learned to guide the great eight-horse teams—the horses matching grays with yellow blankets—through the heavy traffic, carrying loads of brass to the railroad yards and hauling loads of zinc and copper back to the plant. His fellow drivers were mostly men who had driven circus wagons and were full of tales of faraway places. It was, he thought, very pleasant, but then the malarial chills began to come again. He tried to keep on working. As winter came on the chills grew worse. He would break company rules by stopping his team in side streets to go to obscure saloons for a drink while on duty. Wrapping himself in one of the yellow horse blankets, he would gulp down hot rum to break his chill. Finally he could stand it no longer. He did not want his brother and sister-in-law playing nursemaid to him. Winter had come on, bitterly cold and damp, and he headed back for Arkansas where the winters were short and the snows rare. It was the last time he was ever to see the East. He disliked leaving his family, but he did not belong in their world.

He arrived in Heber Springs, Arkansas, in the first days of 1912. Here in the hills, he hoped, the "ague" might be less severe than it was in the bottom lands around Newport.

He no longer had a team of his own and, after paying his railroad fare, had no money—nothing more than the clothes that he wore, his saddle and his box of books. He worked as a hired man, hauling lumber from the mill, lashing new railroad ties into rafts to be floated down the river. He worked as a hand on the small cable ferries that crossed the Little Red River. In season he chopped cotton, thinned turnips, harrowed corn, planted pumpkins in the creek meadows. Anything that needed to be done he would do: making and mending fences, hanging gates, digging cyclone cellars, cleaning cisterns, repairing barrels, hauling water when the wells went dry. He shaved his neighbors and cut their hair, dug graves and buried them when they died. He doctored animals and hauled manure, repaired harness and wagons, broke mules to work. He cleaned and patched his own clothes and, faced with the necessity of living in a series of tumbledown log cabins and boxwood shacks, each more dilapidated than the last, he became a carpenter of sorts. He cut millet, threshed wheat, shocked corn, raked hay. He dehorned and branded cattle, helped handle the stock at horse and mule sales, sometimes traveled around the country with a string of mules to sell for a dealer, seldom making anything above the dealer's demanded price but always enjoying the landscape. He did anything that could be done, with honesty and decency, to earn a dollar or a dinner, and sometimes late at night, lying on a chair pallet with an oil lamp at his elbow, he reread *Pickwick Papers* and *Don Quixote* and wished, hopelessly, for someone to talk to. He would dream of places he had been and things he had seen: girls with shining black hair and bright ribbons in the dusty, dry towns of Arizona; of great, fearsome hounds coursing after wolves in the snows of Wyoming; of a full-rigged Italian sailing ship in Elizabethport when he had gone for oysters and chowder; the deep woods of northern Michigan and the brawling lumberjacks; the purple sedge and yellow-blooming cactus in the sand hills of Nebraska, and the lovely little colts running with awkward speed beside their mothers.

Once, with borrowed money, he went to South Dakota to register for a drawing of government land. And again he beat his way into the Dakotas to work in the wheat harvest. He worked with Wobblies and learned their bitter songs:

> . . . no matter where you're going,
> You'd better stay away.

and:

> Work and pray, live on hay,
> You'll get pie in the sky when you die.

But he could not learn, as the Wobblies did, to blame society for his woes. It was, he felt certain, all his own fault, though he did not understand why. He came from good people who had no complaints against the world, and he had none, either.

He would drift on to jobs in Minnesota, Iowa and Illinois, but always he came back to the hills of Arkansas where the soil was sometimes the color of chocolate, sometimes of snuff and more often the rich red of cinnamon—and darker where the shining plowshare turned its rich dampness to the sun. He had learned to love the blue hills and the morning mists rising from the rivers, running now red and muddy, now green and clear as the days lengthened. He loved the garish brightness of the maples and sweet gums in the fall, but he preferred the spring when the dogwood and Judas trees formed white and pink clouds that floated in the rich, solemn greenness of the woods. Spiky iris bloomed in hedges along the rutted roads, wistaria draped itself around the shaky porches and chimneys, and sleek-sided mules, winter fat, pulled ancient plows in the garden plots. This was the time of year when a man could live on catfish and poke greens and could always get a day's plowing or fence making, when a man could remember with joy what the old Psalm-singer had said: "He sendeth the springs into the valleys, which run among the hills. They give drink to every beast of the field: the wild asses quench their thirst. By them shall the fowls of heaven have their habitation, which sing among the branches."

He was conscious of his daydreaming. When it became so continuous that it interfered with his work, he would dose himself heavily with calomel, and if this failed would take bitter drafts of a terrible brew made of the root of May apples, hoping to purge himself of dreams as well as poisons.

Puzzled by his inability to get ahead, no matter what he tried, he consulted an ancient Negro fortuneteller named Aunt Caroline, who studied coffee grounds in a cup and told him that he would be successful in love, that the lost money would be recovered and that his enemies would suffer. And pointing out that since his birthday was on the sixth, the sixth verse of the twenty-first chapter of Proverbs, which as everyone knew was the birthday chapter for men, held the answer to all his problems. The old woman, unable to read, asked Kelly to read it for her. "'The getting of treasures by a lying tongue,'" he read, "'is a vanity tossed to and fro of them that seek death.'" Aunt Caroline nodded wisely, and Kelly left, no more comfortable for his brief concession to the superstitions of the hills.

Occasionally his parents came to visit him, dressed in their city clothes and bringing his pretty young sister, Margaret, and his younger brother, Philip. Kelly would clean his cabin furiously, borrow bedsteads, featherbeds, oil lamps and a cookstove from neighbors. He would borrow a horse and buggy, would clean and polish the harness, curry and groom the horse so that he could, on Sundays, drive his family to church with a flourish. He would stretch his credit to the limit, buying groceries and supplies. He would take his family on tours of the more prosperous farms in the neighborhood, introduce them with pride to the people he knew. He would take them for outings in the woods and along the river. And he humbly agreed when his father insisted on settling his debts with grocers, suppliers and neighbors. He was always desolate when his family left, and when he could he sent gifts to them: boxes of pecans and hickory nuts, baskets of peaches and apples.

While he maintained a cheerful face for the world to see he sometimes let his feelings show in letters that he wrote: "I am not good enough to be good and not hard enough to be bad. I do not want to harm anybody or anything. . . . Sometimes I feel like sitting down and howling like a dog, and then I see some poor bastard in really bad shape and I feel ashamed." A Christmas letter from home with a five-dollar check for a new pair of boots brought this diary entry: "Sure a fine letter . . . but it gave me the blues to think what fine folks they are and what a failure I am making." And a few days later, when the year ended, he wrote, "I hope to do better next year than this. I aim to, anyhow. Here's five years shot to hell."

Chapter 20

SHORTLY after returning to Heber Springs, Arkansas, from one of his aimless trips, Kelly went to a neighborhood party with a friend, Peter Files, and met Jessie Bowers. Pete Files was interested in Jessie's younger sister, Julia, and Kelly was attracted to Jessie. She was pretty, she liked to listen to him talk and thought his jokes were funny. Her family had come from Tennessee, as had so many others in Arkansas. Her father, like Kelly, had been a wanderer. When Jessie was still a young girl the whole family had packed up and gone to Montana. In time they came back to Arkansas, but Jessie still had the interest in faraway places that Kelly had.

But if Jessie had some of Kelly's spirit of adventure, she also had a practical side. She had been cooking for the entire family by the time she was twelve. She knew how to plow and plant and cultivate, she knew how to can and preserve vegetables and fruits and had a knowing hand with chickens and cows and pigs.

They were married and worked together to make a ramshackle cabin a fit place to live. Kelly worked with a prolonged industry and interest that he had seldom shown before. He hauled cull lumber from the lumber yard where he was employed part time. He built a kitchen for the cabin, roofed it with tar paper, put in a ceiling and a floor, patched the cracks in the walls, hauled pine saplings and old wire and put up fences. His family sent a box of linen and silver and the walnut bedstead in which he had been born. His crops were thrifty and prices good, and within two years he was able to buy a little fifty-acre tract of bottom land near Pangburn. Since both he and Mrs. Kelly suffered from malaria they did not attempt to live in the bottoms to work the land. He planted corn and peas and kaffir and ribbon cane, pumpkins, turnips, squash and melons. He fought off mass onslaughts of ants, crows, moles and cutworms and kept a steady watch on the water that backed up from the White River, through the Little Red River and into the creek that bordered his own land. An overflow was fine before the crop was in, depositing rich silt. But when his planting was done a

93

rise in the creek might rob him of his seed. He cultivated prodigiously, and somehow luck was with him. His crops were good. Jessie, meanwhile, busily raised chickens, tended a cow and had eggs and cream to sell. On rare days off they would go to the river with cane poles and worms dug from the garden patch. Jessie would catch perch for their supper; she was a natural fisherman with nimble fingers and a sure instinct for setting the hook. Kelly enjoyed it but preferred to lie on the ground staring at the sky while the fish stole his bait. In the spring he frequently saw flocks of wild geese high overhead, tingled with excitement at their faraway honking, thought of the flat green rice fields to the south where they had been and the deep blue lakes of the north where they were bound. But for once in his life he did not have the urge to hit the road. The sun was warm, the earth promising, the crops good, his home comfortable—at least by his standards, and the future was bright.

Occasionally he and Jessie would both be stricken with the aches and fever of malaria, but they managed to keep going. Kelly farmed his own land and rented more from others. He was up and ready to plow before daylight. He cleared brush and cut fence posts. On rainy days he busied himself with making the house more habitable. He gambled with the unpredictable river and planted every inch of a sandy island in the stream bed to corn and happily saw it make a crop. He split up a white oak tree that had fallen by the river and, working at night with a spokeshave, converted it into almost twenty dollars' worth of wagon wheel spokes to be sold in Pangburn. He shot squirrels and ducks for the pot and delighted in the meals that Jessie fixed— squirrel pie and fried fish, cornbread with cracklings, bowls of clabber and crisp radishes and onions, slabs of home-cured ham and chicken fried so that only the thick crust kept the meat from falling off the bones, poke greens, new potatoes, peas and beans, and apple pie with heavy cream and spicy cakes with sweet icing. And on Sundays, when Kelly had time to haul a chunk of ice from the icehouse in town—a chunk he himself may have cut from the river the previous winter—they would make thick ice cream to have with their cake.

On trips to the feed store in Pangburn, Kelly would weigh himself on the feed scales. Strangely, his weight stayed just the same, 165, but this was only because he was working harder than he ever had before.

He had never lived so well nor felt so full of energy and purpose. In dollars and cents he was little better off than before, but gradually he began to accumulate property: a mare and then a colt and then a team of sturdy, stubborn black mules to do his plowing; a sow and then a pen full of pigs; a cow, a calf, a steer for fattening; a yard full of Plymouth Rock chicks.

He rented more land and, swept along by the wartime boom in cotton prices, became a cotton planter. It was not a crop that he liked, but that was where the money lay, and landowners were reluctant to go into renting or cropping deals unless the renter or cropper agreed to put the land to cotton. Cotton was readily marketed, easily stored and could not be eaten by the producer as could other crops. Kelly rented more land, four acres here, five acres there; borrowed money at the bank for seed and to pay the pickers. He made money, substantial money, for the first time, even with cotton prices falling. But he watched with dismay when cotton prices fell to ten cents and less, puzzled over good cotton going so low. He had farmed as well as he knew how; he had worked as hard as a man was able to work; and his cotton was graded high—he almost always topped the market. Still a man went broke this way, and if he had his way about it he never would be broke again. His early prejudices against cotton returned. What he really wanted to be was a stock farmer—a little dairy herd, some cattle, hogs, horses to breed and raise and train. But to do it he must have a money crop.

Again and again he told Jessie of the High Plains in the Texas and Oklahoma Pan-handles—the magical country he had seen that morning from a caboose in Dalhart, Texas. Great wheat crops had been made there during the war years. A man could go there, have a few good years in wheat and set himself up in the stock business; the country was perfect for cattle and horses. Jessie agreed. Kelly sold his creek bottom land at a little profit and sold the crops that still remained in the fields. He crated up the brood sow and delivered her to a neighbor. He scraped the rust from his farm implements, painted them bright red and traded them to a friend for a little traveling wagon. He soaked the wagon bed in the creek to tighten the joints, cleaned and painted it, and built a feed and baggage boot for the rear. They disposed of the household goods that were too large to go in the wagon, packed up the walnut bedstead, boxed Jessie's sewing machine and Kelly's books, wrapped the old saddle in gunny sacking and packed a box with jars of preserved vegetables and fruits.

Early in November, 1921, they set out on their journey. The mountain woods were lovely, the oaks russet, the pines and cedars deep green, the sycamores ghostly white, the sumac rusty red and the maples crimson. They left the strange flat-topped mountain of Heber Springs behind and passed one familiar landmark after another, the Post Oak

Missionary Church and Foster's chapel, the old white-pillared mansion at Mount Vernon. They camped in creek bottoms where there was water and grass for the horses—the Panther, the Gar, the Big Mulberry and the Little Frog. The mountain ridges flattened out into rows of hills and the hills disappeared into wide, grassy plains. Now and again they glimpsed the wide Arkansas River, flowing low and clear in the autumn months between yellow fields where prairie hay had been cut. When their day's journey ended in a big town they stayed in wagon yards. Here travelers and their horses stayed together. If they were lucky there would be not only stables and feed and water for the horses, but a cookhouse where traveling families could prepare their meals, a shop where a horse's shoe could be nailed on, occasionally private rooms for families if they did not sleep in their wagon. Some were comfortable, refined, a social and business center for all the country around where women could gossip and men could talk about the wheat crop in Kansas, the cotton in Arkansas and what in hell had happened to cotton prices, work in the Oklahoma oilfields, the land that could be bought cheap in the High Plains, the fruit crops far to the west in California, where there was work for harvest hands the year around.

Others were simple and primitive, little more than camps. At one the proprietor said to Kelly, "Hell, man, you mean to tell me you got a woman in that wagon with you? You better git her right out. There'll be a hundred teams in here tonight and it ain't a safe place for no woman."

They stayed in Tom Carlock's wagon yard in Morrillton, Elmer Smith's yard in Van Buren—the largest wagon yard Kelly had ever seen, the Old Texas yard in Fort Smith, Graham's yard in Sallisaw, the City wagon yard in Checotah.

Kelly loved the wagon yards and the life that went on around them, and as they drove West in the shortening days he told Jessie of the many he had stayed in, and how wonderful the wagon yard had been in Phoenix in 1904 when he and his brother had walked down into the desert from the mountains.

"I never will forget my first night in that town," he would say. "Phoenix has always been a good town. We went to a wagon yard. That's where your work comes and goes. There was the Okay wagon yard and the Silver Dollar yard and the Five points and lots of others. They had bunkhouses there where you could roll your bed down and stay, or if you liked the open air you could throw some straw under a wagon and sleep there. It was just damned nice. Every yard was full of freight teams. There might be four, six, eight, ten head of jerkline horses, hitched to a freight wagon. They'd come in. Then the prospectors would come in with great long strings of burros. At periods during the night those burros would start to bray like all donkeys do. Then over yonder at the Okay wagon yard they'd all pipe up, you know. The burros in each wagon yard would wait for the others to get through before starting their own little symphony. It was very nice. There'd be a different pitch to them. They can really make a noise, just shake the earth, but when you're off a way it's quite pleasing. They've got a tone to them. Like roosters.

"And we'd see those old freighters coming in there to Phoenix after a long trip across the desert. The driver would be setting up there on the near wheel horse, scratching himself. Crummy, you know. And damned near asleep. They were pretty, though, you know, those long strings of horses and mules. All different colored animals. Pintos and bays and buckskins, and sorrels, and black mules and white ones and old snuff-colored mules with mealy noses. Quite attractive. And sometimes a long string of wagons traveling together for comfort and safety and aid. They might have rough places where they'd double up, pull one another out. It was a very nice life."

More and more automobiles passed them on the road, speeding by at twenty and thirty miles an hour, kicking up great clouds of dust, spraying mud out of the chug holes, frightening the horses. Kelly would curse them, trying to calm his horses, but he knew that the automobiles would some day drive the horses off the road and would some day make the wagon yards obsolete. Wagon yards were spaced at distances that horses could cover in a day. When men covered greater distances by automobile the wagon yards would disappear, and Kelly didn't like the idea.

He would, he told Jessie, some day paint her some pictures of the wagon yards and the way they had been, the way he had known them. "Do that, Kelly," she would say. She never called him anything but Kelly. Kelly had not made many pictures in the last few busy years. But Jessie Kelly always carried with her five tiny pictures of trotting horses that Kelly had made for her and given to her when they were married.

Some days they covered twenty-five miles or more, some days none at all. As they moved westward across Oklahoma the weather worsened. There were torrential rains. Then the wind would whistle out of the north and there would be snow. They crossed wide prairies and, climbing gradually, came out on the high, windy plateau of the Panhandle. They arrived in Perryton, Texas, on Christmas Day, after a journey of nearly eight hundred miles in fifty days. They marked the holiday by going to a rodeo, and on the next day Kelly had a job as a hired man on a stock farm.

This was the country he had longed for, but somehow it was not the same as he remembered it. Much of the rich sod land had been broken for wheat in the time since he had seen it. The country was flat and empty and cold. The wind never dropped. Sometimes it piled snow deep in the miserable roads, and at other times it would bring great clouds of choking dust; a dry norther would roll up yellow-brown billows, scouring loose dirt from the furrows the plows had made.

Miserably lonely and cold, they struggled through the winter. Finally, in March, the barren landscape began to show green; a few birds sang, frogs began piping and the wind died down a little. The coal fire in the kitchen stove stopped smoking and was allowed to go out. The Kellys celebrated by going to Wolf Creek for a picnic. Jessie caught a pail full of little fish. Kelly, as usual, lay on his back and stared at the sky and thought of the farm he would like to have here some day. A small herd of Durhams, some mares that had the speed of thoroughbreds and the sturdiness and all-around usefulness of the quarter horse; a registered quarter-horse stallion; the crops of colts that he would train and sell; sturdy mules to pull the big plows you needed in this country; a creek where cottonwoods would grow to protect the stock from the searing sun and the biting wind; an orchard, a vineyard. . . .

He had rented a little piece of land to farm on his own, but his oats and wheat and barley were poor; there was barely enough to pay the rent. Jessie was ill, their capital was gone and finally Kelly borrowed sixty dollars on his team of horses to get them back to Arkansas by train. Here they stayed for two more years, Kelly once more working as a hired man at any odd job that could be found, helping at the sawmills, driving other people's teams. They rented another tumbledown house and Kelly went through the same things again—adding a kitchen, putting in a floor, patching the roof, digging out a spring. They reclaimed some of the old furniture they had left behind and things were the same again except that they were a little older and no longer owned any land. Their daughter Martha was born, and both of the Kellys enjoyed being back among their friends in the hills. They lived frugally, saved what money they could and by August, 1924, they were ready to go back and try Texas again.

Chapter 21

WHEN Kelly returned to Texas from Arkansas he was forty years old and was ready to begin a new life, preferably one of more accomplishment and less aimlessness. Work was plentiful for a capable hired man. He worked with harvest crews, did plowing for hire, drilled grain, cultivated, built fences, hauled water. He broke, harrowed and seeded an entire section for one man, driving a team of eight bad-tempered mules for as much as thirty miles a day, unable to make them stand long enough to permit a drink of water or a smoke; at night he would listen to the landowner's complaints about the shortness of the day, and finally he would jerk with exhaustion in his sleep.

In his second year he was able to contract to buy a quarter-section of land south of Spearman. The land was flat and the soil was deep and rich, and it was of a size he could farm by himself, using horses and mules. He did not want to farm with a tractor, as most men now did in the Plains. With a tractor, Kelly held, man was at the mercy of a machine. If you knew horses, knew how to work them and care for them, nothing could happen to you. Farming was a natural way of life, and horses were a natural part of farming. You could raise feed for horses; you couldn't raise gasoline or kerosene for a tractor.

He bought an abandoned farmhouse for twenty-five dollars, razed it and hauled the lumber to his new land, building a new house from the wreckage of the old. He salvaged more lumber from abandoned dugouts that people in the Plains had once used for shelter, and built sheds and outbuildings. He hauled sand from a creek bed to mix with cement. He broke his land, planted grain fields and garden patches, set out a little orchard, but kept enough of his land in grass to graze his stock through much of the year.

The first year on the new land was a hard one—a dry year, a year of hard freezes and burning heat. The Kellys ate jackrabbit hash and hauled spongy cottonwood logs from the dry bed of Adobe Creek and gathered cowchips to burn in the stove through the long winter. Unable at first to have a well drilled on his place, Kelly hauled water in barrels. But gradually things improved. Rains came and grain sprouted and flourished in the soil that could be incredibly productive under the right conditions. When his grain crops came in they came in such quantities that he had to hire help at harvest time. He bought back a favorite mare that he had had to sell during the first abortive trip to Texas. He bought other horses, a milk cow and pigs. He bought a secondhand Model T Ford, and on Sundays he took his family for drives, down over the Cap Rock and into the breaks of the Canadian River, past the great Turkey Track ranch, past the old Adobe Walls battleground, where first Kit Carson and then the buffalo hunters had fought the Comanches, Kiowas and Cheyennes.

Good year followed good year, and by 1929 Kelly was convinced he needed a larger farm. Some of his neighbors, similarly hungry for more land, were moving up into Dallam County, the northwesternmost corner of the Texas Panhandle. Land there was still cheap. The sod land, once broken by the plow, was rich and could, with a little rainfall, produce big crops, and almost everyone was talking big crops—whole half sections and sections planted to wheat.

But Kelly was not thinking of big single crops. He wanted enough land to be a substantial stock farmer; grassland enough that it could be grazed in rotation; and only enough cultivated land to raise feed for his stock, vegetables and fruits for home consumption, and enough cash crops to provide his family with some comforts. He would like to have an entire section, but failing that he needed at least a half section. He knew something of the vagaries of this land and thought he could control them. He would never, if he could help it, cultivate more than half his land; stock would be his mainstay. He would breed and raise and break horses for sale; this was work he liked best, and he disagreed with his neighbors who said the tractor would drive the horse from the field as surely as the automobile was driving him off the highway. He would have shorthorn cattle for both beef and milk; and pigs and chickens. He would introduce perennial legumes that would enrich the soil, hold it in place and fatten his stock. He wanted to become a self-sufficient farmer with the kind of independence he had always dreamed of.

In the fall of 1929 Kelly sold his land at Spearman at a good price and went looking for land in Dallam County, and when he found, east of Texline, a half section described on the county books as the east half of section twenty, seven FDW, he thought it was what he had always been looking for. It was the kind of land he had seen from the lookout of a caboose in 1904, the kind of land he had wanted ever since.

It was a slight depression in the high, flat country, what Plains farmers called a "valley," although it was little more than a faint wrinkle on the bald face of the country. A dry creek bed crossed it in a southeasterly direction. The land sloped ever so gently to the arid watercourse, but the depth, at its greatest, was no more than a few feet below the level of the surrounding tableland.

It was part of the great flat apron that spreads eastward from the rough eminence of the Rocky Mountains, a country with a bleak beauty and vestiges of a strange and varied history: seashells from the ocean bed and the fossilized bones of huge, grotesque animals that had come to the increasingly scarce waterholes to drink and kill or be killed; ancient men who had tilled the soil and fled the country as it became drier and drier, and less ancient men who were hunters, pursuing the great herds of buffalo that blackened the land as far as eye could see. Coronado and his helmeted men had marched across this country, looking for the Gran Quivira. Then there had been cassocked priests and the *ciboleros* and *comancheros*, traders and freighters, soldiers and desperadoes. Here the Indians had first watched with anger and then resisted with fury as the tide of white men swept across their land, slaughtering the herds of buffalo on which the Indians lived, killing not for meat but only for the hides, leaving the carcasses for the carrion eaters and the sun and the wind.

The land that Kelly chose had once been a part of the Buffalo Springs division of the famous XIT ranch. A syndicate of wealthy men had built for the state of Texas a pink granite capitol in Austin and had received, in payment, a grant of more than three million acres of this land, a tract more than two hundred miles long and extending through ten counties (hence the name XIT—ten in Texas)—more land than Texas had given to veterans of her war of independence and the Civil War combined. Cattle counted by the thousands grazed the land. Buffalo Springs was the northernmost of the pastures and the coldest; here yearling steers were brought to condition for summer pasture in the more rigorous climate of Montana.

The day of the great herds came to an end and the great ranch was broken up into parcels, some sold to ranchers of less magnitude, more of it to speculators, promoters and developers, who were gambling on the growing American hunger for new land and the undying hope that in a new country the opportunities would be greater for coming generations. Special trains brought in the customers, some eager, hard-handed farmers from Illinois, Iowa, Missouri and Kansas, ready to break the sod land and make crops; merchants and bankers ready to invest. Land agents in linen suits and panama hats met the special trains. Frame hotels were erected almost overnight to accomodate the newcomers. Early automobiles had been brought in both to impress and transport the prospects, great high-wheeled vehicles that bounced over the prairies, frightening jackrabbits, prairie chickens and the occasional antelope and wild horse. The land agents were eloquent, painting pictures of golden fields, mounds of fruit, heavy vines and pyramids of melons. Land was bought and sold and plows cut up the tough buffalo grass sod that had been centuries abuilding, and the range land became a country of feast and famine, of dreams and disillusion. High wheat prices and adequate rainfall made fortunes; dry years and a weak market brought bankruptcy. Land was tilled and abandoned to cactus, thistle and tumbleweed. Those cattle that remained in the country overgrazed the narrowing pastures until the grass roots were gone, and the plows churned up the soil until the ancient humus disappeared; a dry year and the unending, scouring wind would set the whole countryside in movement until ocher haze blotted out the bright blue of the sky and the high, fluffy clouds.

When Kelly found the land he wanted it was all overgrown with blue weeds, salt grass and thistles. He could correct this with proper care. The creek bed hinted at shallow water. Old neighbors from Spearman were to the east and west of him. They had bought their land at fifteen dollars an acre. As a latecomer he had to pay eighteen. But he had made a good profit on the Spearman farm and could afford it. He contracted for the new land at a time when the stock market was collapsing in spectacular fashion. Such things were no concern of his; his values were different: they were real—rows of tender green breaking through well-tilled earth, fat pigs, cows with great udders and bawling calves, mares in foal, their sides round and shining, trees in bud and flower and fruit, the fine geometry of well-kept fields, the pleasure of a garden with onions, cabbages, turnips and potatoes, and pumpkins turning golden in the stubble. He was a farmer and a stockman, not a gambler who played with pieces of paper.

He contracted to have a well dug, a windmill erected and a tank put up for stock. He hauled new, unused lumber from the yard to build himself a house, a better one than he had ever had before, with ready-made windows and doors. He started on the house March 24, 1930, put up plates, studs and joists, got rafters in and the sheathing on and decided, at the end of one week, that it had begun to look like a house: a living room here in the center where he and Mrs. Kelly would sleep (some day they would build a separate bedroom for themselves); a little room on the south for their daughter, Martha; the kitchen on the north where the heat of the stove would do the most good; a little porch on the east side, facing toward the creek. Here, in the summer when there was no early plowing to be done, he could sit and watch the sun come up across the plains, watch the colors shift and change, grow and fade—all on his own land.

He plowed a garden and truck patch, disked his oats and planted milo maize, made a hog lot, fenced a yard for the chickens, set out potatoes, planted corn, bedded little bare-root locust and ash saplings in the yard and Chinese elms along what would, some day, be a shady lane leading to the road. Cherry, plum, peach and apple trees went into the orchard. Cottonwood switches were stuck in the ground along the creek bed to grow into trees and temper the wind and shade whatever moisture there might be; it would, in time, be a cool place for cattle to drowse when the summer sun was straight overhead. He ordered more shade trees from a nursery in Kansas, as well as a dozen each of gooseberry, currant and rhubarb plants and one hundred grapevines. He set out tomatoes and peppers; built roosts and shelters for the chickens and glazed the windows in his house. He went to Clayton, New Mexico, and bought a new bonnet for Jessie, an Easter basket full of cotton rabbits and chicks and jelly beans for Martha, and a new Stetson hat for himself. He contracted for a second well and windmill in the pasture.

In the evenings he liked to look out over his land, listen for the cry of the curlews, and think of the day when his own stout fences would cast long shadows at this time of day, the grain high and golden in the slanting sun, the trees cool and green, moving a little with the wind; bright flower gardens around the little house; the vines heavy and the trees in the orchard bowing to the ground under the weight of their fruit.

Chapter 22

FOR nearly ten years Kelly struggled with his Texline farm. These were the middle years of his life, a time when men erect monuments to their energy and sagacity, build their last homes, carve lasting marks on the earth, plant saplings that become great shelter-giving trees, form friendships that are a comfort in old age and acquire those things that are generally thought to bring both security and serenity.

Yet, at the end, there was little to show that Kelly had ever been near the half-section of land in Dallam County. For his land was in the very heart, the dead and desolate center of the region that people learned to call the Dust Bowl. It was a pear-shaped blot on the map, its thick section spread across Colorado and Kansas, its tapered stem ending near the Rio Grande. Kelly's farm was where the core of the pear would be, a place where the winds were the wildest and the dust thickest.

The house that he had put together with his own hands became no more than a heap of lumber.

The fences that he built became the unseen vertebrae of sand dunes.

The clean, straight furrows that he plowed became only slight irregularities in the wind-scoured surface of the land.

The trees and hedgerows, he planted became dry, brittle sticks.

The wildflowers that he had dug from the pastures and planted around his house to relieve the flat gray-brown monotony of the landscape became dust without having cast seed.

His friends and neighbors died of "dust pneumonia" or scattered east and west across the continent. Kelly himself was almost the last to leave the empty country where everything seemed to dissolve and became part of the sand and dust that moved back and forth as relentlessly as the tides of the sea.

And, Kelly thought, it was like the sea in its great emptiness and its levelness—

and its violence. The wind swept up the loosened earth and piled it in nightmarish windrows, like great coastal dunes. And the successive waves of the wind, like the waves of the ocean, carried things along, buried them and, again, cast them up. Just as a stormy sea will gouge out the shore and disclose shells and bones and ship's timbers long hidden from man's view, so the wind in the High Plains uncovered the past: a strangely wrought piece of brass, thought to be an old Spanish stirrup; old gun barrels and branding irons with curious, unknown characters; flint points the Indians had used to kill the buffalo and harass the white man; horned skulls and giant bones, scoured white; wagon wheels (the oaken spokes made excellent firewood), worn and broken but perfectly preserved in the dust that had buried them. Tools and implements that Kelly himself had lost or mislaid would remain hidden for years; then, with a shift in the wind currents, they would magically reappear with no trace of having been excavated.

There was always a perverse fury to the weather. Kelly had heard old settlers say that Comanche medicine men had placed a curse on the land when the white man had killed the last of the buffalo, driven out the last of the Indians and, as they said, turned the earth upside down with a plow. It was, they said, a curse that would make it forever unfit for the white man. Kelly did not believe in curses or hexes or magic, but he conceded that if witchcraft existed this land seemed to be bewitched. The wind was violent and unpredictable; a southerly breeze could, in a moment, change to a violent southwest wind that unroofed houses and flattened sheds. Or it could swing into the north, and in minutes a balmy day would becoming a freezing one. Lightning would illuminate the whole sky, from horizon to horizon, and thunder was always an explosion that shook the earth. Hail came with stones the size of hen's eggs, capable of striking a man to earth. The rains were scarce but when they came they were furious. Pounding the earth where all vegetation had disappeared, they rapidly formed torrents. The dry creek bed that crossed Kelly's land could, in moments, become a millrace, muddy water carrying everything before it, drowning chickens, washing seed from the ground, uprooting the little trees that he tried to make grow along the banks.

But of all the furious aspects of nature the dust storms were the worst. Kelly had known dust storms before, but never anything like the storms that came to the High Plains in the thirties. The whole heart of the continent was blowing—land in New

Mexico, Colorado and Wyoming that had been overgrazed; the sand hills of Nebraska where ambitious men had tried to plant row crops; the cornfields of Kansas and the great grazing lands of the Oklahoma and Texas panhandles, where men had ripped up the ancient sod, trying for quick fortunes in wheat.

Several times in the first spring on his new land there were severe storms. Huge yellow clouds would appear on the horizon and there would be a dry, peppery smell to the air. Seeing the cloud and smelling the air, Plains people headed for home as rapidly as possible. When the storm closed in, they knew, it would be impossible to see. People became lost in the storms. If they could they found a fence to follow, running a hand slowly and carefully along the top strand of barbed wire. Some became confused and panicky and died of suffocation. The blackness came quickly, and the brightest lantern was of no help in the suffocating gloom.

This, Kelly told himself, was to be expected in a dry spring and, at first, it did not alarm him. His own land retained moisture well and he was not plowing enough of his land to run the risk of it blowing away. Still, the dust that blew from the overgrazed and overcultivated land all around him drifted onto his own land, burying the new grass in the spring, leveling the furrows he had plowed, choking the new growth in his grain fields.

Wheat prices had dropped almost out of sight, and with them the demand for the things Kelly had hoped to be able to sell—colts and calves and pigs. One by one his neighbors began preparations to leave, "the women a-weepin' and the men a-packin'," as they said. This one's land was ruined. That one saved only a few bushels of wheat, not worth hauling to town. This one's children developed asthma and heart trouble from the dust. They went back to Missouri, back to Arkansas, or hopefully struck out for California.

Kelly puzzled with them over the mysteries of economics.

"Now I take a load of corn into town," one would say, "unload it, and pick up a load of coal and they give me a credit slip. I look at it and it's just for a few goddamn cents. I think there's been a mistake, but the man says no, that's the way it is. Corn is cheap and coal is dear. So I come home and I look at the corn I still got in the barn, holding back to feed the pigs. And I look at the pigs; I can't get two bits for them. So I tell my boy we'll just kill the pigs or give them away. There's no use pouring good corn into them. We'll just burn the goddamn corn instead of coal. And that's what we're doing, by God, although it seems sort of peculiar, sinful like."

And:

"I made a right smart crop of milo maize, right at twelve hundred bushels, which is pretty good considering the dust and the drouth and the bugs. I took it in and got my money and then went to the bank to pay off my seed note, eighty dollars, and when I got through I didn't have enough to pay off the threshing crew for helping me. I still owe them. Now how's a man gonna get ahead? Harder you work the farther you fall behind, and what I want to know is where you gonna end up?"

Kelly didn't know the answer, but he went ahead with his own work, building shelters for his stock, plowing and planting the same land again and again, hoping for the right combination of rain and calm, dust-free days to produce a feed crop for his stock. On nights when there was no dust in the air he painted the interior of his house, praying that the dust would not fly before it dried, hung doors and put in a ceiling to cut off the wind that swept through the rafters.

Jackrabbits came, at first by the hundreds and then by the thousands, to nibble at any green thing that managed to force its way through the drifted dust. Kelly borrowed a gun and killed them as fast as he could, hating to do it. But the rabbits came in increasing hordes. He poisoned some maize heads, put them out for the rabbits. One of his best horses got into the poisoned grain and died in agony. Grasshoppers swarmed in and ate what the rabbits left. His cattled died from grazing on thistles. Two more horses died of a disease vaguely diagnosed as dust fever. He scrimped and borrowed in order to feed and doctor his stock. He took newborn calves, colts and pigs into the house to protect them from the dust until they could gather strength.

He overdrew his checking account and discovered that the cash balance left from the sale of his earlier farm had dwindled away. He fell behind in his taxes and mortgage payments on the new farm. He borrowed money at the bank to get seed for the future and feed for his stock. He packed up one of his treasures, a collection of old Currier and Ives prints, and sent it to his younger brother in the East to sell for him. He bartered with his neighbors, a shoat for a barrel of coal oil or a few sacks of coal, a bundle of hay for a piece of harness, a crate of frying chickens for help in fixing the windmill. He registered with the county commissioner for work on the roads and occasionally got a day's work for himself and a team of horses, leveling out the dust on the roads that would stay level only until the next gust of wind. He did not like charity, but the fact that he was functioning as a horseman and a teamster was a mitigating factor.

It was not Kelly's nature, however, to be chronically unhappy, and he found pleasure in many things. His neighbors, most of them in worse trouble than he, were fine people, and their miseries drew them closer together. They shared their troubles and their food supplies, sat up with each other in illness, had musical evenings singing sentimental ballads and favorite old hymns. They held church services in the district school, had box suppers and, in the occasional periods of fine weather when the sky was blue and clear and the air invigorating, they went on picnics.

Jessie Kelly's garden, watered by hand, seemed to do well in spite of the dust—although sometimes the wind would blow so hard she would harvest beans and peas for canning by picking them off the garden fence where the wind had blown them. They always had food, and there was seldom a Sunday that some of their neighbors did not come to eat with them.

After eating, Kelly and the men would walk out in the fields and stare at the ruined landscape. Here the top strand of a wire fence would be only inches above the drifted soil, then it would disappear altogether. In places the earth would be swept bare down to the clay hardpan, as impenetrable and sterile as any city pavement.

No one understood Kelly's attitude toward his stock. He petted his cows, babied his colts, carried on long colloquies with them, and they followed him around the place as a dog would, nuzzling him, begging for more attention. He brushed and curried his horses after every dust blow, just as Jessie Kelly tried to keep the dust swept out of the house. He knew his friends joked about it but did not care. He would show them the old one-eyed stallion with the broken ear, as gentle as any kitten, and the roan Durham bull. He would walk up to the bull, brush the dust from his sides, scratch his head.

"What you trying to do, Kelly," his friends would ask, "make a watch fob out of that brute?" Sometimes the bull would push Kelly against the fence. "That bull'll kill you one of these days. Makes no sense to baby a bull. Bulls take kindly to only two things—food and cows."

Kelly would explain, "You handle a bull gently and talk to him so he gets to know you, then you can lead him around and show him like you would a horse. It makes a good impression with the people if you want to sell him."

His friends would laugh. "Who's going to buy a bull these days? A bull or a horse or anything else? And how they going to pay for it?"

Kelly did not know.

A few of his neighbors still kept horses, but it was largely a matter of sentiment; few of them were worked any more, and with feed prices high they were rapidly disappearing. This was tractor country. A man's only hope of making a living in this fickle country was to plant big. If the crop was big and the price high, a man could get rich in a year or so. If the price was low but the crop big enough, a man could still make a little money. The way to get a big crop was to plow and plant every acre you owned, and a man could do this only if he used a tractor and the big gang plows. To harvest such a crop you needed a combine, and to keep up with a combine you needed a truck to haul your crop to the elevator. You could not keep up with a combine with horses and wagons. They all liked to talk about a city fellow named Hickman Price, who had gone into wheat farming in a big way. He owned much land and bought and leased more until he was farming nearly thirty-five thousand acres, all in wheat. He bought tractors by the dozens, ran fleets of trucks and combines, had machine shops to keep his equipment working and motorcycle messengers to serve as high-speed couriers between his various operations. His great gang plows, pulled by big tractors, broke up as much land in minutes as a man with a team could do in a day. The fact that Hickman Price had gone bankrupt did not lessen the appeal of the type of farming he was doing. Most of Kelly's neighbors were committed to the tractor, the combine and the truck, and almost all of them were in hock to the implement dealers. The dealers had begun importing high-powered collectors to try to get something out of the hard-pressed farmers and a small-scale guerrilla war followed. Some of the farmers hid out from the collectors, some stared them down, some assaulted them bodily. One collector was chased away with a razor, another had the lobe of an ear bitten off in a fight; others were peppered with birdshot.

Kelly sympathized with his neighbors but he joked about their involvement with the implement dealers.

"If you wouldn't fool around with those damn tractors and had stuck to horses, you'd be all right, just like I am," he'd say.

"Yeah," they'd answer. "Well then, how about letting me have five bucks till I get my crop in?" And they would all laugh as only men in trouble can.

Kelly tried to go through the motions of farming. He would excavate his fences, take up the posts and wire, then drag the dunes with heavy timber to try to get the land back to its normal shape so that it could be cultivated. He would move fence lines only to have new dunes build up wherever he put the fence. He tried to follow the advice of the soil conservation people. He plowed on the contour, but after the next blow no trace of his efforts could be found. He bristled when a young government man told him that what he really needed was trees to provide shelter and retard evaporation. Kelly was tempted to tell him of the hundreds of trees he had set out, but he remained silent.

His cattle wandered away, walking over the drift-covered fences, and he spent much of his time chasing them.

Gradually he was reducing the number of his livestock. He sold calves and pigs to the government to be destroyed, shaking his head over the insanity of it. He let cows go at ridiculous prices, and marketed chickens at prices that would not cover the cost of gasoline to get them to town.

He even tried reducing the number of his horses. But instead of selling them for whatever they would bring, as he did with his other stock, he usually traded, trying to end up with fewer but better animals. Sometimes he succeeded, sometimes he did not.

He talked with everyone he could about other places to farm: deep east Texas where the land was rich and the climate humid; the Rio Grande Valley, where irrigated land produced tremendous crops of fruit and vegetables and cotton.

He took a trip into northeast Texas, into Fannin and Lamar counties, and shopped around to see if anyone was interested in trading forty acres of that good black waxy land for a half-section in the plains. People laughed at him.

He tried, unsuccessfully, to sell the equity in his land to the Rural Resettlement Administration.

And he watched the skies for rain. Sometimes there would be showers "just over east or south of us," and he offered silent thanks for his lucky neighbors. But on the few occasions that rain fell on his own land it came in cloudbursts, cutting great gullies wherever there was the slightest grade and carrying away the little humus left in the soil. Drying, the soil packed hard under a broken crust, like badly applied paint, with weeds sprouting in the cracks.

Somebody stole his good Cheyenne saddle. With a neighbor he tracked down the vagrants who had, he was certain, taken it. He found his lariat rope in their belongings, but the saddle could not be found. The men were arrested but acquitted for lack of evidence. Somewhat later he traded a promising colt and a few dollars for another saddle. It was a Miles City saddle, and had belonged to an old horseman who came through the country each spring, breaking horses at ten dollars a head, work which Kelly always did for himself and friends. He had admired the old man and envied him, wishing he could make a living the same way, but to do it a man had to travel all the time. You couldn't do that with a family. The Miles City saddle was a good one, but somehow it never quite replaced the Cheyenne saddle that had so long been his proudest single possession.

Chapter 23

IN one spring the town of Dalhart, Texas, reckoned that sixty-six deaths had been caused by "dust pneumonia."

Albert Law, reporter for the Dalhart *Texan*, attended a meeting in Guymon, Oklahoma, of representatives of the four states most affected by the dust storms. He wrote of some of the things he had seen and heard.

"Not a blade of wheat in Cimarron County, Oklahoma. Cattle dying there on the range.

"A few bushels of wheat in the Perryton area against an average yield of four to six million bushels; with all the stored surplus, not more than 50 per cent of the seeding needs will be met.

"Ninety per cent of the poultry dead in one Panhandle county because of sand storms.

"Sixty cattle dying Friday afternoon between Guymon and Liberal from some disease induced by dust; milk cows going dry, turned into the highways to starve; hogs in such pitiable shape that buyers will not have them; humans suffering from dust fever.

"Cattle being moved from Hartley and other counties to grass. No wheat in Hartley County; row crops a remote possibility; cattle facing starvation.

"Potter, Seward and other Panhandle counties with one-third of their population on charity or relief work.

"Ninety per cent of the farmers in most counties have had to have crop loans, the continued drouth forcing many of them to use the money for food, clothes, medicine, shelter. . . .

". . . [there is] imperative need of millions of dollars now to save livestock so that human life can be sustained and the productive agencies of the Panhandle snatched from obliteration. Estimates are from 45 to 60 counties and 60,000 families must have help at once. At $250 per family to last the humans and livestock a year, the total is $15 million. . . ."

A college president pleaded: "These people only ask a chance to earn. They have built this country. Our government, in helping them, is not giving but investing in a section that is a big portion of the nation's bread basket. We think it humanitarian when our government sends money to earthquake-torn Hawaii, to feed destitute Belgians, to save the Armenians. Are we to stand idly by and see our fellow citizens starve to death?"

And, in Washington, President Roosevelt asked Congress for an emergency drouth relief appropriation of $525 million: ". . . the situation has become more grave as the rainfall shortage has continued. Future rainfall cannot restore more than a small part of the damage to crops and livestock."

Kelly described the disaster in more homely, personal terms in a letter to his parents:

"We've had some terrible blows. The roads are impassable in many places for sand drifts. The other day when Jess and I were dog-hunting we stuck the Ford in the sand six times. We carry a shovel along and dig out. We sure stay home at nights. The school tried to have a box supper for two different Friday nights and a blow came each time and stopped it. Little Martha had such a pretty box fixed up. Well, we ate the contents at home anyhow.

"Do you realize that when a blow comes we cannot even see the barn? The air is that full of dust. Sometimes it blows three days on end.

"It must be healthy dust, though, or we would have died long ago. I dragged our best cow off the other day. She had been 'sanded up' for a month or two. I drenched her with linseed oil and fed her good, but she finally died anyhow. Her calf we put on another cow—two red calves on the same cow.

"There is a government man working on our case here. The President's idea is to move people out of the marginal farm territories. We would have been moved out last year but for Alfalfa Bill Murray [of Oklahoma] and Governor Allen [of Louisiana] putting up such a howl. They don't have to live here and see their stock drying up before their eyes, trying to find a bit of grass under the dust. When we get a little squirt of rain, the Dalhart paper talks like all our troubles are over. It stops the dust for a couple of weeks.

"There is a strip 'most two hundred miles wide from the Rio Grande to the Canadian line that is now practically a plumb desert. If they want to help us to land in east Texas, why not take it? They moved 2,500 families, stock and machinery, out of west South Dakota into the east part of that state.

"If it rains here to bring grass this spring, all right. We will have no wheat at all. There is a little south of Dalhart, a little around Texhoma, none at Spearman. The whole Panhandle is a desert now, sure enough. Central Kansas has wheat, but the plains all the way north and south are dry.

"If they give us a chance to go I aim to go down on the coastal plain on the sandy land next to Louisiana and milk cows and raise feed for them. It has to rain soon or this country will be abandoned anyhow, and I don't aim to quit and walk out with nothing. It is a very worthy project, moving people out of here. We ought to hear something pretty soon about moving. I am not worrying. I like it here in normal times, but I am outstaying most of the fellows at that, so can't be called a quitter. And I am not going to swamps, rocks and hills when I leave. There is fine grass and fruit country in north of Beaumont in the cutover pine plains, like south Jersey. It would be a nice country to winter in. Well, time will tell, and that pretty soon. The towns are against any talk of wholesale moving, and one can't blame them. However, they are soon going to have to dig us farmers out to find us. People don't know how things are by reading the papers. Each Chamber of Commerce boosts its own town even if it is buried in sand so you can't get to it.

"It is all in the hands of God whether we stay or we 'exodust out.'"

There was a great hopelessness about everything. Spring after spring Kelly tried to do some plowing, resolved that he could no longer wait for the wind to fall and the dust to settle. When he reached the field with his plow and team the wind would begin driving again; furrows disappearing as rapidly as he could make them. The dust was blinding and choking. He attempted to plow with his head swathed in wet cloths, but he would give up out of consideration for the horses. The men in the neighborhood tried to hold meetings at the schoolhouse to discuss their plight, but as soon as they gathered the dust would begin flying thicker than before, forcing them to hurry home while there was still enough light to find their way. Salesmen were touring the country with patent rainmakers but were doing very little business; no one had any money. Special church meetings were held to say prayers for rain, but the men said, among themselves, "There's no use in bothering the Almighty about rain when the wind's in the southwest." West, north, south—all winds were dry, and dusters, as they had begun to call themselves, claimed they could tell the origin of a storm by the color of the dirt in the clouds—if it was yellow it came from Texas or New Mexico, if brown, from Kansas, if red, from Oklahoma. And Oklahoma dust, they claimed, tasted worse than the rest.

The spring months were the worst, but sometimes there was a respite. Sunday, April 14, 1935, was that kind of day. It had dawned warm and pleasant, the air clear for a change, a strong suggestion of spring in the light breeze. Kelly worked around the farm all morning, doctoring his stock, pulling tools and pieces of harness out of the dust. In the afternoon his wife and daughter went into the fields to see if the wind had uncovered any more arrowheads. Kelly poured hot water in a washtub and took a long, soaking bath, scrubbing himself with a stiff brush until his skin was tender, trying to rid himself of the ingrained dust. He washed his graying hair and shaved twice, once with the grain, once against. He rubbed Red Arrow liniment on his face; the burning of the liniment gave him the feeling that he had really shaved, something he had little time for any more. He put on a clean blue work shirt, pulled on his trousers and threw himself on the bed.

He sat up with a start. It was dark. He was not conscious of having slept and he looked at his watch. No more than a half hour had elapsed. He sniffed at the air and knew that another dirt storm was coming. He ran to the door of the house. The sky in the northeast was an ugly, muddy color from horizon to zenith. His wife and daughter were running across the fields, trying to reach the house before the dust became blinding, suffocating and deadly.

Kelly hurried to the pasture and drove in his horses and cattle. By the time he returned to the barn it was dark as any night. He lit a lantern but it gave only a feeble yellow glow in the gloom. He tied the horses to a rail and put the cows in a lot with their calves, letting the calves suck, although he had been trying to wean them.

Running his hand along the top strand of the fence, he groped his way back to the house. He helped his wife and daughter hang quilts over the windows and doors. Outside it was as black as a moonless, starless midnight, although it was not yet six in the evening. Mother and daughter went to bed, pulling sheets over their heads. Kelly wrapped a wet towel around his face. He lit the gasoline lantern. Its usual white glare was a faded yellow in the dust. He sat and stared at the wall; dust sifted down it in patches, like fine-ground flour in a grocer's bin. Outside the wind kept up a continuous moan, but otherwise there was complete silence. The dust had a way of deadening sound.

There was always a tenseness during the storms, and Kelly found it impossible to sleep, and the silence, except for the whining of the wind, was oppressive. It was, he thought, as if the country were completely dead, completely empty. And it might be that before long. His neighbors were leaving, one by one: back to wherever they had come from, or heading west toward the supposed wonders of California where there were crops the year around, where a good farming hand could get all the work he wanted and good wages too. There was never a week that "movers" did not come by Kelly's place, often stopping to inquire the way. With the drifted dust all roads looked the same, and it usually was impossible to tell direction by the sun, hidden in the murky sky. Usually they wanted to "trade" for some eggs, lard or bacon, too, and Kelly would trade with them although he seldom had any use for what was offered. But eggs taken to town would bring only ten cents a dozen; it was hardly worth fighting the dust to take them in; he might just as well give them away.

Often Kelly would read through the whole night, his eyes watering and stinging. He might doze, but he usually awakened with a feeling of suffocation and would go on reading, sitting in a straight chair by the gasoline lamp. He brought books from the library in Dalhart, books of travel and geography, with pictures of rich grain crops on the Russian steppes and the Canadian plains, gauchos riding after fat cattle on the pampas of Argentina, stands of timber in the Central American jungles, the rice paddies of the East with workers and buffalo standing in the water.

He often thumbed through his Bible and read Job over and over again ("I am full of confusion . . . a land of darkness, as darkness itself; and of the shadow of death, without any order, and where the light is as darkness").

He read *Moby-Dick* and thought that he, in the heart of a continent, knew some of the things felt by Ishmael in the heart of the ocean ("And meet it is that over these sea pastures, wide-rolling watery prairies and Potters' Fields of all four continents, the waves should rise and fall, and ebb and flow unceasingly; for here, millions of mixed shades and shadows, drowned dreams, somnambulisms, reveries; all that we call lives and souls, lie dreaming, dreaming, still; tossing like slumberers in their beds: the ever-rolling waves but made so by their restlessness").

He would turn to the first book he had ever bought, when he was sixteen and eager

Hilltop Dance Hall

River Ferry Crossing

to become a horseman and a farmer, Magner's *Standard Horse & Stock Book*. He would leaf through it again, smiling each time he read the pretentious title page: "All secrets of taming, controlling and educating unbroken and vicious horses, with details of breaking up all habits to which horses are subject; their abuses, diseases and remedies. Also: Full description and illustrations of the various breeds of cattle; sheep raising; swine and their diseases; the poultry interest; the dog and his ailments; bee culture; fruit culture; grafting; insects injurious to fruit, etc. And a plea for birds."

Magner was good, Kelly thought, but somehow he failed to touch on what to do when stock had, for too long, been breathing dust and ingesting it with their food. And he overlooked the various things that could happen to stock when the owner just couldn't pay for the kind of feed they needed.

And he would, again, pick up a translation of Marcus Cato on agriculture, a curiously knowing old book that he had once found in a secondhand shop. He would reread: "and when they praise a worthy man their praise took this form: 'good husbandman,' 'good farmer'; one so praised was thought to have received the greatest commendation. . . . It is from the farming class that the bravest men and the sturdiest soldiers come, their calling is most highly respected, their livelihood is most assured and is looked on with the least hostility, and those who are engaged in that pursuit are least inclined to be disaffected."

And he went on to read Cato's specifications for a good farm. The neighbors should keep up their places. It should have a good climate, not subject to storms. The soil should be good and naturally strong. It should be well watered and it should, if possible, lie at the foot of a mountain facing south. It should lie among farms which seldom changed owners.

After a time Kelly's eyes would tire. He would reach in a drawer, pull out a harmonica, tap it gently on the table to rid it of dust. He would lower the towel from his face and, eyes closed, knees propped against the table edge, would play old country dance tunes so softly that the music could barely be heard above the complaining wind.

Chapter 24

KELLY was a diligent diary-keeper. As a child in upper Michigan he noted in a shabby little notebook his earnings on a paper route and his trading and breeding of rabbits. As a young man he kept a faithful record of his far wanderings, how he had gone from this place to that, what he had earned and how he spent it, the arrival and departure time of trains, the look of the land and, always, the state of the weather. There were occasional notes of accomplishments and disappointments, of pleasant en-counters with girls, of bouts of conviviality and the distress that followed, of the speed of certain horses on half-mile tracks, of the little pictures he had drawn and to whom he had given them. But there was always a laconic impersonality to it. He recorded the evanescent and trusted his memory to hold the more worthy, memorable things. When he married his only diary notation was: "Married at 6 P.M. Big rain at night." He did not, in the cramped notes he kept in a succession of notebooks, unburden himself. He did not exercise the secret, subjective arrogance of "literary" diarists, did not indulge in rationalization, speculation or reasons why he did what he did. He noted the titles of books he had read but seldom the exultation, fascination or sorrow they gave him. On very rare occasions he gave a hint of misery, but in the next line he would go on with his prosaic, objective observations: "Cloudy, but faired off late."

But men seldom record what they intend to record. The most laboriously written diary may prove the exact opposite to what the writer had hoped to establish. Kelly intended his diary as a mere daybook, a record of transactions, of farm tasks done and needing to be done, of livestock bred and born, sold or died. But, somehow, he managed to convey much of the suffering of the Dust Bowl years, the horror and hopelessness of the weather, the sorrow and despair of his neighbors, the increasing loneliness of an untenable land and, inevitably, the flashes of unexpected pleasure that relieved the monotony—bright-colored little flowers blooming in unlikely spots, wild fowl pausing in their migrations, the solemn joy of people praying and singing hymns together, the warm pleasure of homely gifts that impoverished people give one another—a bag of onions, a chunk of side meat, a sack of popcorn, a bottle of tepid, yeasty homemade beer.

1931

Saw Mr. B. at bank about money to pay interest and taxes. Says yes. Sold boar pig for ten dollars' worth of corn. . . . Forty-seven years old tonight. Whipped-cream cake. Shaved. Jess washed and got some wild-flower plants from pasture. . . . Faired up. Shoveled snow. Went to Coldwater singing in P.M. Big crowd, string musicians playing "Sweet By and By." Was grand. . . . Hauled manure for hot bed and spud patch. Burned weeds around lower mill and had time fighting fire. . . . Set out cherry, plum, locust and ash trees. Big sow had ten pigs. Five chilled before day. Old sow had twelve. Put two with big sow. Harrowed off oats on fall plowing to kill thistles. . . . Got Chinese elms for grounds, set out over one hundred. . . . Mrs. H. had twins, boys, one dead. Neighbors all up there. T. and I sat up all night. . . . Baptizing in W.'s pasture in P.M. Twenty young people from Perico. Grand sight, and fine old hymns. . . . Plowed sod. . . . Planted corn, pumpkins, hegari. . . . planted beans . . . planted milo in north field. Seven shots, six rabbits. . . . planted milo. It is sprouting on far side. Eight shots, eight hits. . . . planted soybeans. . . . Pasture in P.M. to see ducks, Jess, Martha and I. Bright has a red roan heifer. Five daughters now and two granddaughters. . . . Crops good. Raked hay. F has fine patch of melons, sweet corn, cucumbers. . . . Last day of summer. Need rain . . . rain in early A.M. Good inch. . . . Cold, misty. Looked like a freeze. Pulled pumpkins and Jess pulled tomatoes and butter beans. . . . Gathered corn, hauled in hay. . . . Sow has seven pigs . . . sow has nine pigs. . . . Old Bright is sick. . . . Blaze sick with colic, died at night. Eleven years old last July 2. . . . Snowed. Pete and I took hogs to Clayton, sold at three sixty-five. Paid bank fifty, got overalls, gloves, socks, shoes for Jess, coal. Pete had some fine beer. . . . Threshed . . . took rest of milo in, paid off bank, feed store, paid Pete for help hauling. Letter from home. Ten dollars for Xmas.

1932

H. has left out. Left his stock for the bank. . . . First curlews of the year. Grass is greening. . . . Cold blow from northwest. Air full of dust till sundown. More dust in the house than we have ever had. Miserable day. . . . Still have north wind. Listed in field where barley blew out. S.'s barley blew out too. Wheat looks sick. Sure hard luck. . . . Claude G. packed up and left. Brought their cattle over here. Set out more Chinese elms along drive; Jess planted more cottonwoods along creek. . . . Bank putting out no more money for a little while. . . . Applied for federal crop loan, one hundred dollars . . . borrowed Dan's little gun to shoot rabbits for the hogs to eat. . . . Big blow and sandstorm from the southwest. . . . Cream ten cents, eggs six and seven. . . . Finished planting kafir and harrowed off ten acres of corn. Sure a dusty job in west wind. . . . Made shed for sow and fixed hog-lot fence. Planted spuds. Came in as cloud rose in southwest. Big rain. Some hail. Water from garden ran into chicken house, drowned seventy chickens. Sure sad. . . . Weeds are sure growing. . . . H.'s have sold out. . . . Nine cents for forty-eight test cream! . . . Traded Pete a shoat for a barrel coal oil. . . . Jess made Martha a new coat out of John's old overcoat. . . . Dragged old Slim off to pasture, my third horse to die this year. . . . C. has sold out. . . . Threshed. Got about fifteen bushels kafir. Made six loads of milo. Very thankful for what we have. Many folks had no grain at all. Paid Jake four pigs for helping thresh. . . . It looks boogery in north but clouds are beautiful. . . . Harrowed thistles west of our house. Pete and I burned them all. Tired at night although it is work that I like. . . . Faired up. Went to town. They are working the streets with needy men. Cream eighteen. . . . Xmas barrel from home with lots of clothes, shoes and things. Also good letter. . . . Christmas Day. Martha got me up at midnight. Found her doll and then kept me up till daylight. D. here for dinner, with peanuts. Gave him a pair of Mr. S.'s shoes. Fine ones. . . . F. here. Traded him sow pig for work on car, seven more pigs for three tons of corn.

1933

Letter from home with check for taxes. . . . Big blow from southwest. Out again with lister but had to quit. Couldn't even see. Blew terribly all afternoon. . . . Looked at wheat. Plowed ground is buried but alive. Guess most of disked wheat is gone. . . . P. has no feed left to spare. . . . Big flock of geese went north. Ducks on the creek. Got three mallards for Jess. Don't like to kill them but she is duck hungry. . . . Didn't plow on account of cold, windy and dusty. Set out apricot trees. Watered newly set trees. . . . Another southwest blow. Finished plowing P.'s garden for him before wind got up. Plowed furrows along west line of our orchard and planted *bois d'arc* seed for shelter hedge. Also along north line of stomp lot. Came in out of dirt. . . . Cream sixteen, eggs eight. . . . Have new holder for mouth harp and I play nearly every night now with harp and guitar. . . . Covered wagon went by. Nice team. Boy and sunbonnet girl on saddle horses. . . . Jake left, for Enid, Okla. Bid him good-by and good luck. Planted two acres corn in north field. Southwest blow again. . . . To town for groceries and cough medicine. Terrible southwest blow. . . . Took eleven roosters to town. Two cents a pound! . . . Harrowed oats ground and drilled but had to come in account of big dirt cloud. . . . Big rain at night. 'Who giveth rains upon the earth and sendeth water upon the fields' (Job 5:10). . . . Took eight pigs and four shoats to J., traded for two barrels of coal oil and some seed to come. . . . Saw Mr. B. at bank. They will carry me on. Cattle dying of bloat from grazing on thistles. Dirt blew from southwest in late afternoon. . . . Cream only thirteen cents. . . . One cow died, another sick. Bloat. . . . Took ten hens to town, sold at six cents, $2.49. Cream fifteen. . . . Martha broke arm, falling off burro. John W. set and bandaged it. . . . Package from folks and check for coal. Martha had good day but cried at night. Cultivated spuds in north field. Read to Martha and played store with her. . . . Newt and I drove to Mt. Dora, N.M., for coal, got two tons at the mine scales. Saw Santa Fe trail monument. All a beautiful grass country, and cedar on the hills. Timber in the valleys, too—cedar, piñon, ash oak, cottonwood and pine. I miss trees. . . . Federal Land Bank appraiser here. . . . Land bank granted $3,200 on this place. . . . Went to town, got ten dollars for expense money. . . . We all went to Dalhart to sign deed of trust to land bank. . . . Went over to B.'s to get order for Red Cross clothing. Went to Dalhart and got examined for relief work. . . . Worked on county road . . . the timekeeper brought out a sack of treats for each man. . . . Christmas Day. Rev. B. and Mrs. B. here for dinner. Nice visit and music and singing. They are fine singers. . . .

1934

Worked on road. We work seven and one-half hours each day at thirty-five cents an hour. Twenty cents more with team. . . . Bird has a fine horse colt. White stockings behind and a big star. Looks like a roan prospect. He had trouble locating the teats as her bag was so large. Jess finally got him to sucking in late afternoon. I did not get much plowing done. . . . Misty and cold. Cleaned horse stalls. Hauled manure to garden. Old Bright has a blocky red heifer calf. Her eighth heifer. Good old Bright. . . . Hard norther set in at midnight. Blew until noon. More dirt than ever. Then a fine snow until late afternoon. . . . Made new note at bank. Eggs eleven, cream twenty-one . . . dug up cottonwoods at well, all except big one, and set them around tank. . . . Southwest wind. Listed in north field. Can't wait for wind to quit this spring again. . . . Starting to blow. J. and I started to Dalhart but stopped by the dust. Sold seventeen dozen eggs at ten cents. . . . Southwest wind. Movers stopped by. Gave them a little side of meat and three dozen eggs. Nice young men with wives and small children. Going back to Kansas. . . . Ben K. died of dust pneumonia. . . . P.'s shack blew away. Helped him pick up stuff. . . . Fanny Fern has black filly colt. White star and tiny snip. Old Spot has eleven pigs. Dirt storm from southeast in late afternoon. Cream twenty, eggs ten. . . . Children's day at church. Good program, ice cream and cake afterward. Played with Ed and Rev. B. on violins, Melvin, George and myself on guitars. I played harp also. Anna played mandolin and Elmer tenor banjo. Played "Sweet By and By" and "Leaning on the Everlasting Arms," in C. . . . Got into the damnedest dirt storm ever, from southeast. Home just before dark. Sat around looking at soil maps and atlas. . . . Young Henry S. died in doctor's office. Heart failure. Very sad. . . . P. and family left for Oklahoma. Helped them load truck. *Vaya con Dios*. . . . Church at night. Good sermon. Your sins will find you out. L. pulled R.'s house by here. . . . Y. is moving out. Got coal oil from them. . . . Borrowed ten dollars from Slim. Interest people here after L.'s machinery. . . . U.S. buying cattle to slaughter. Sold them four calves, $13.85, to pay off bank. Then brought calves home and dressed them. . . . Saw land bank man, made livestock mortgage for feed loan. . . . Letter from Dad with check for Xmas. God bless them. . . .

1935

Good old Bright has a red heifer calf, tenth calf, ninth heifer. . . . Ed is going to Kansas to work in a garage. This settlement loses a good man. . . . Palmer, Slim and Earl all went to Colorado, land-looking. I scattered manure. . . . Day set for state fasting and prayer by Governor. Big southwest blow. . . . Letter from Father with ten dollars for birthday. . . . Got $80 feed loan check. Paid off $81.98 feed bill. Scattered manure in garden. . . . Newt and I to Dalhart to crop and feed loan office. They're sure busy. Big southwest blow, worst we've had. Stuck in sand. . . . Newt and I to Felt, Okla., to look for secondhand plowshares. Not many people left around there. . . . Wind blew all night from north, cold and dirty. . . . Fair and warmer, clear. A little grass greening along the fence. Bobolinks here now. Four quail near the hen house. . . . They got a fine rain near S.'s place. Good for them. . . . Up to Slim's to borrow disk harrow, Jess, Martha and I. Met two Gray County chuck wagons with remuda and two thousand head of cattle. Showed them how to get over to Coldwater Creek for water and grass. Had pressing invitation to dine at chuck wagon. Cook said, "You owe it to that girl." Disked near home in afternoon. . . . Talked to H. about going to east Texas. . . . Rode after cattle near artesian well and looked at bunch of horses. Found some white gentians. . . . C. out. Gave me $55 for Black Annie, Dutch, Gracie and two calves. . . . John S. and son here, sold them Daisy and Bird cows at $30 per, Grace heifer at $20, and red calf at $10. Sent $90 check to bank at Dalhart. . . . Larry K. out to look at stock. Traded him Blackie, Nelly's filly, for use of his field for pasture. . . .

1936

Dixon out to look at horses. Bought Sis and Belle for $200. Hate to see them go. . . . Went to town. Paid feed bill. Got oats and cottonseed cake. Bought medicine and some things for Jess. . . . Hell of a duster out of the north. . . . Southwest blow. Couldn't do anything. . . . Southwest blow. . . . Norther on. Lots of dirt piling up. . . . Blow from northwest starting at 3 A.M. Blew hard all day. Lots of dirt. Out of sugar and sirup. . . . Tried to plow. Quit on account of dust from north. . . . Contour plowed pasture but norther ran me in. Sure dusty. Letter from Pete. Their wheat is gone. . . . Used team to pull tools out of dirt. . . . Dragged dirt away from garden fence. Ernest gave me a sack of feed. . . . Jess and Martha walked in fields hunting arrowheads. . . . Dragged dirt from barn. . . . Cleaned sand out of garden and around well. . . . Shower at night. Frogs piping over south. . . . Jess and I to town to get garden seed. Saw our mares, Belle and Sis, and their colts at Dixon's. They are sleek and fat. . . . All hands to Dalhart. Country looks good. Teams in fields, plowing. Took Martha to Dixon's so she could see Belle and Sis and their colts. . . . Planted eight rows of sixty-day milo in north field. Went to S.'s sale. He's leaving for California soon. . . . Set out some more trees in yard. . . . Bright has roan heifer calf. . . . Bobby and Queen have red bull calves. . . . Sold Dandy to Newt for $50 and the promise of fifty acres' plowing. . . . Queen cow died at 2 A.M. Her bellowing awakened us but not in time. Dragged her off to pasture. . . . Young S. has sold out. Traded Dolly and ten dollars to him for his white mare. . . . Thanksgiving Day. Ground sausage and rendered lard. Bird mare lost her colt. . . . Traded three bull calves to S. for good Jersey cow. . . . Ed left for California. Good luck to a good man. . . . Gave Martha her little wrist watch for Christmas and sent her to bed happy. . . .

1937

Wind boxed the compass. . . . Black duster from north. Used masks. . . . Newt, Stub and I went to rodeo on the Cimarron. Grand trip, fine country, good rodeo stock. Saw a bloody bay stud I'd like to run. . . . Went to Clayton. Borrowed $20 from B., got two sacks of oats, bale of hay and two teeth pulled. . . . Sold Bobby and calf to Z. for $25. . . . Broke Jack to drive and then rode him. Fine ride. Watered flowers. . . . Z. bought spotted calf for $12.50. Two answers to my newspaper ad to sell this land. Helped Jess peel peaches and wrote to land-buyer prospects. . . . Sold header for $50 and barge for $5 to Cecil. . . . Larry and Sam out and bought Jack and Daisy. . . . Bud out to buy Jiggs. . . . Henry S. down to buy bull, $60. Cattle are off again. . . .

1938

Young and Crump here and got old Kingpin. Going to send the bay horse down to the sales. Traded black horse and Lizzie filly for six-year-old 1,500-pound bay stud. . . . Cold and dusty. Norther on. Brought in some more wagon wheels for fuel. Blew all last night and blowing tonight. . . . Dragged roads, or rather dragged sand. Northwest blow drove us in. . . . Southwest blow. . . . Terrible southwest blow after noon. Found a wrench I lost three years ago. . . . B.'s here for dinner and nice visit. Sure hate to lose them as neighbors. . . . Regular downpour at dark. Three inches in one hour. Saved all the chicks but one. . . . Over at schoolhouse at night for ice-cream farewell party for H. They are going to California. . . . Some New Mexico people here looking for W. He left out long ago. Some Dalhart men inquiring way to Clayton. . . . Some others inquiring way to Buffalo Springs. . . . Grasshoppers and drouth are denuding pastures and crops. . . . Sold roan heifer to E., $45. . . . Amarillo man by, showed him the place. . . . Some Fort Worth men by, looking at land. . . . L. by at noon. Tried to sell him the place. . . . Southwest blow. Tumbleweeds moving. . . . Norther blew up but cold rain at night laid the awful dust. . . . Cecil by to look at place. . . . S. looked over place. . . . K. here to look at place. . . . Sold bull to S., $40. . . . My lost glove blew out from under coal bin. Some luck, anyhow. . . . Southwest blow, weeds and dust. . . .

K., the feed dealer, bought small heifer at $65, way above market. Paid him $9.25 for balance of feed bill. . . . Got stuff ready to move. Truck came and loaded up and pulled out above 2:30. S. came for chickens. Left home at 4 P.M. Cold, and some snow on ground. . . .

So ended Kelly's own version of the most disastrous chapter of his life. None of the prospective buyers of his land was really interested. It was reclaimed by the Federal Land Bank. Then, miraculously, there came a year of good rains. The grass came back, crept over the hummocks and dunes, anchored the restless soil with its roots, and it once more began to look like the magical sea of grass Kelly had seen from a cattle train long years before.

"If I could have stood it a couple of more years I might have been all right," Kelly would say. "In '41 they had better than forty inches of rain in that country, where we'd been trying to get by on ten and twelve inches, and my land resold for almost three times what I paid for it. Or, if I'd left earlier I could have got a little something for it. I might have got away without losing my shirttail and all the fixtures. I didn't even get a road stake. I just had to walk away and leave it for the bank. It wasn't hard, though. There was almost nobody left in that country. We were almost the last ones to leave except for some Mennonite farmers. I remember what one of them told me. 'Well, good-by, Brother Kelly,' he said. 'If I don't see you again in this world, I'll see you in the next.' That was nice, wasn't it?

Driving a ten-year-old car that wheezed, rattled, groaned and barely crept along the highway, Kelly left the country that was flat and endless, gray and bleak in the middle days of February. He went south across the High Plains, down across the Staked Plains, over the Cap Rock and into the rolling prairies of west central Texas where, God willing, a fifty-five-year-old man might make a fresh start.

His heart had a murmur. His lungs had so long been clogged with dust that he was certain, at times, that he was suffocating. But his eyes were bright and his spirit tough. He was no longer a landowner. But if he had to be a renter, he would be a good renter. The little farm he had leased near Blanket, in Brown County, seemed to offer at least some of the things the past had denied him. It was only 160 acres, just half as large as his farm at Texline, but with a little luck he might rent a larger place in another year or so. Or even buy one.

Chapter 25

THE air was clean and sweet. Kelly remembered now how it was to smell things other than the wind-driven dust: a barn full of prairie hay; the damp richness of a pecan thicket along the creek where the poke greens would grow; the old-time smell of wood smoke, and of frying bacon; the pungency of moist ground turned with the plow, the curls of earth shining like the plowshare; the good, rank smell of tawny piles of sheep's wool in the shearing shed.

On all sides there were little low limestone hills with mottes of dark and tangled live oak, clumps of mesquite, lacy green, groves of sycamore, hackberry and Spanish oak, of post oak, cedar and cedar elm with flocks of sheep and goats moving slowly among them. This, the Cross Timbers, was a country that had a beginning and an ending, unlike the emptiness of the plains. Water drained down from the springs in the hills and formed a creek that wandered through the valleys, keeping the bottom pastures green through much of the year. In the mornings there would often be a cool fog between the hills, and sounds carried pleasantly in the damp air, the squalling of a top horse, the bad-tempered racket of a boar pig trying to get through a fence, the tinkling of turkey bells and the first clanging sounds from the blacksmith shop.

Everywhere there was an air of permanence, and this pleased Kelly. Families had been here for generations. Their grandfathers and great-grandfathers had come here and driven out the Comanches and had stayed to work little ranches and farms. The land was neither rich nor vast. No one became very wealthy, but then they seldom went broke, seldom left. The soil was thin and poor, but a man could get by. There were good years and bad years, but the good years were not so far apart. A man could live from one to another. The climate was bland. The winter months were short, and while the summers were hot, trees and water tempered the heat. Men kept horses, rode them to look after the stock, hitched them to plows and cultivators to work their small fields. They raised corn and maize to feed the stock, cotton and peanuts for cash, chickens, turkeys and pigs, a few grade cows, and there were pecans to be gathered by the sackful along the creek.

This was the kind of country Kelly had longed for in the Plains, friendly, peaceful, self-sufficient.

The farm he leased was, he found out too late, worn out with too many row crops. The barn was falling apart and the house was little better. Jessie Kelly wept silently when she saw it for the first time. In their first spring on the new land a cloudburst washed out the grain Kelly had put in, and a windstorm flattened the old barn. Neighbors came and helped him pull his old stallion out of the wreckage, amazingly unhurt, and then stayed on to help him build a better, stronger barn out of the lumber of the old. His landlord gave him an allowance on the lease for rebuilding the barn, and neighbors helped him to shore up and strengthen the sagging house, got the windmill in running order, brought wagonloads of wind-fallen wood for the fires. Their women came with pies and cakes and helped stuff mattresses and make quilts. When Kelly tried to thank them he would choke up and be unable to speak. He was loyal to his old friends in the Plains, but they had never been like this; they had all been too preoccupied with crises of their own. The people here were settled, established, confident that everything would be all right. And they were particularly helpful to anyone who had come from the dusty Plains. When Kelly would speak of the dust storms the men would shake their heads and stare at the ground.

His wife and daughter would often go in the evening to visit with neighbors. Sometimes Kelly went with them, but if he could do so without offense he preferred to stay at home. If the night was warm he liked to sit in front of the old house and watch for the lights to come on in other people's homes. It made the night a thing you shared with others, not a dusty blackness that you endured by yourself. He could look at the stars again and enjoy the soft blackness of the sky. He could hear the sound of trucks and automobiles on the state highway, bound east for Fort Worth or west for Brownwood and Angelo, see the flash of their lights as they crested a hill. Occasionally there would be scraps of music in the night air and the sound of people laughing and sometimes the sound of hounds bugling back in the hills on the trail of a coon. These were all warm, pleasant things. Often he would place his hand on the earth, damp and cool in the evening, and with his fingers trace a wandering strand of Bermuda grass, feeling how firmly, at intervals, it rooted itself. In the darkness he would hear the call of a screech owl and would think how misnamed they were; that theirs was really a pleasant sound. And he would remember how he had once found a tiny screech owl near the hen house, popping its beak and frightening the hens, although it was barely able to fly. He had picked it up and put it back in a tree and his friends couldn't understand why he had not killed it. An owl was a varmint and you killed varmints. Kelly even liked the larger, fiercer hoot owls and regretted the few times he had had to kill them. He had had many arguments with his friends on the subject of predators. Although he had no liking for wolves and coyotes, he did not like the way his neighbors in the Plains had hunted them down, pursuing and shooting them from a truck. If there was a right way to do it, he thought, it would be to run them down with horses and dogs. Nor did he like the way some men caught thieving snakes by embedding a fishhook in a egg and waiting for the snake to swallow it. Every creature, he thought, should have a chance to get away. Time and again Jessie had called him to kill a chicken snake, a skunk or coon or hawk; he would get his rifle, go to the hen house, fire the gun in the air and chase the marauder away. He felt guilty about this. He should not, he knew, have any qualms about killing anything that molested Jessie's chickens and turkeys. They were bringing some cash and it was the only cash the Kellys had. This was not the way he would wish it, but this was the way it was.

If Kelly had been disposed to let poverty worry him, he would have been deeply disturbed. But whatever worries he had about his livelihood were outweighed by the pleasure he took in his friendships.

Ernest Allen, who ran the drugstore, was as bookish as Kelly himself. He was almost blind, and it had been a long time since he had been able to read with ease. But he remembered books and discussed them with Kelly and loaned him things he had not read. So did old Eli Crisp, the retired blacksmith who had come originally from Howell County, Missouri, where Kelly had once been skinned in a horse trade. Eli was quiet and pious, but he liked his books with "plenty cuttin' an' shootin'." Doc Yantis and Doc Cobb were both book readers and had books that Kelly had never read.

When he was able Kelly liked, on a Sunday, to saddle up and ride out with Ed Nabors, a lean, spare, quiet man who had a good farm south of Blanket. Between themselves they called it pasture worship: riding through the pastures, looking at the lambs and the new colts. They said very little but, Kelly thought, it gave pleasure both to themselves and to God.

He would do the same with Elvin Williams who had a goat ranch on Salt Mountain. Williams was a vigorous, handsome man who reminded Kelly of a favorite uncle of his childhood. He kept hounds, waged a relentless war on bobcats, foxes and rattlesnakes and was, Kelly discovered, a left-handed roper from Giles. Sometimes they would, after a ride, have a nip of whisky in the barn, but more often they would sit on the porch and eat ice cream or, in season, slabs of cold watermelon. Williams liked to listen, and Kelly would talk of the places he had been and the great horses he had owned, ridden, dreamed of breeding or merely seen.

He became a close friend of B. J. Stevens, a rawboned, red-faced horseman who was just Kelly's age and who led the kind of life Kelly would have liked for himself. He did a little farming and a little ranching, but his main interest was horses and he had the knack of making money with them. He always kept a good stallion and made more from stud fees alone in a season than Kelly had ever made in a year of farming. He always had a few good mares and handsome colts and he never missed a horse sale within two hundred miles. B. J. had a ribald sense of humor and liked beer as well as Kelly did. When he took a horse to a sale or brought one home he usually had Kelly with him, and Kelly loved him for it.

Kelly came to know that Beck-the-blacksmith—Kelly never referred to him as anything but Beck-the-blacksmith—had the same taste that he, Kelly, had for strong cheese and lively stories; and that Pete Krischke could make smoked sausage that tasted just like the sausage his grandfather Osman had once made. And that Sam Diaz, a Mexican, was one of the community's most respected citizens; that his whole family, from very old to very young, worked as a unit shearing sheep and goats and pulling cotton. And that old Lee Stewart, well up in his eighties, still rode his horse every day and rode well. Kelly called him "Kid" and Stewart called him "Old Man Kelly."

He became a friend of Dick Teague, who suffered from asthma, and Jesse Sanders, the blind man, and Louis Tackett of the border patrol, and Red Oliver and Clem Edwards and George Eoff; there were so many.

They all liked Kelly's stories and jokes, his reminiscences about the many parts of the country, and they had great sympathy for the hard time he was having. While some of them watched, one day, Kelly walked out of the Blanket State Bank. The wind was blowing from the northwest, and there was a dusty haze in the air. Everyone knew there was a dust storm in the Plains, where Kelly had come from. Kelly pushed his hat on the back of his head and squinted into the wind.

"Blow, goddamn you, blow," he said, apparently talking to himself. "You made a renter out of Kelly." The watchers laughed. Old Kelly, they said, was always talking to his horses. Now he was talking to the wind.

He was not doing very well as a renter. After a few years he gave up on the 160-acre farm and rented one just half as large, thinking it might be easier and more economical to handle. It was worse, and Kelly gradually became aware of what was wrong. He himself was worn out. He would put in a crop, wear himself out in doing it and take to his bed, shaking with chills and fever and feeling the old choked feeling in his chest. Recovering, he would go back into the fields and work twice as hard as before, trying desperately to catch up, exhaust himself and take to his bed again. He did not like to admit it, but he discovered that he could not stand much physical activity. The slightest chill would bring on a heavy chest cold, and each spasm of coughing would, he said, bring up "about a half-acre of the best dust in the Plains." His heart was strained and his lungs were subject to any vagrant germ. When a cold spell drove him in from his fall plowing he told Doc Cobb, "You know, Doc, what old Solomon said? 'The sluggard will not plow by reason of the cold; therefore shall he beg in harvest and have nothing.' That's me, all right. It's just fine, you know, for a man with plenty wives, horses, horsemen and chariots like old Solomon. The old sonofabitch had time to think up proverbs for other people. He didn't *have* to plow."

Doc Cobb would laugh, prescribe some pills and give Kelly a bundle of old copies of the *National Geographic*.

Finally he gave up the eighty-acre farm and moved to a much smaller place south of Blanket. It could be called a farm only because its location was rural. It had no land at all. There was a ramshackle barn and a dwelling that had once been a chicken house but had, after a fashion, been converted. Kelly, with typical optimism, wrote to his family in the East that it was "snug, light and warm," neglecting to say that it took almost a month of work to make the roof stop leaking during a series of January rains. But their needs were modest now, Kelly thought. Their daughter had married a good local boy, Drew Eoff, and had two fine sons of her own. His own needs were few. He began rebuilding the old barn so that it would accommodate the horses and cows that he still kept as the last shreds of his dream of being a stock farmer.

He had no land of his own to work, so he hired out to others, plowing, cultivating, heading maize, cutting corn and cane, threshing peanuts, raking and baling hay, making fences, shearing sheep, loading wool, vaccinating cattle. Money he made this way, between periods of illness, was barely enough to buy feed for the horses and cows he insisted on keeping. Some day he would make another start as a farmer, he thought, and these horses and cows would be his beginning. If only he could get a little ahead, he would make it yet. He continued to breed his mares and got as much joy as ever when they produced colts—although he knew the price he could get for the colts never paid for the feed and care that went into them.

If Jessie had not been working, it would have been hopeless. During the last years of the war she had worked in the laundry at Camp Bowie in Brownwood. When the camp was closed down she went to work picking turkeys in the meat-packing plant. Kelly did not like it. It didn't look right for a man to be staying home while his wife went off to work, and besides, it was lonely during the day. Jessie urged him to get rid of the horses and cows; if they didn't have to buy feed for them they could get along all right.

But what would he do if he no longer had his stock to look after, Kelly would ask. A man just didn't stay at home and do nothing, did he?

Why, Jessie said, he could paint pictures. Everybody always liked the pictures Kelly painted and gave away. Maybe people would buy them.

Kelly shook his head. He wasn't an artist. He was a horseman and a farmer, who just happened to paint for amusement.

But as the feed bills mounted higher and higher, he agreed that something had to be done. Early in December, 1946, he sent two of his mares to the sale barn in Brownwood. A buyer for the soap factory paid eighteen and nineteen dollars for them. A friend bought a third mare. At the end of December a local rancher bought the last of his cattle, three cows and two calves, for $250. Kelly paid out all of it on old debts and borrowed ten dollars to pay his January rent. By the end of January he had sold his last two mares (they were heavier and brought a total of forty dollars from the soap factory) and his old disk plow for ten dollars. He had held onto them until the last; he might be able to get some work spring plowing, and it would give him an excuse to keep the mares. He now had neither farming equipment nor farm animals, and he had never felt so miserable in his life. He would sit at night in the wretched house and stare at the rough board wall that still had traces of whitewash from its days as a chicken house and wonder what had happend to his life. Everything he had worked for was now gone, and he thought of the many opportunities he had let slip through his fingers, all the mistakes he had made, the land he had owned and lost, the money that he had never been able to keep. He could blame no one. His family had always helped him—far more than they could afford and more than he had any right to expect. Jessie had worked as hard and harder than he had to make a success of things. He had a loving daughter who had never given him a moment's worry—as he had his own parents. He had two fine grandsons. Would they, in time, look up to him and admire him or think of him only as a failure? He had had, always, good friends, who had helped him, who had shared his problems as well as his joys. And now at the age of sixty-two, almost sixty-three, he had nothing to show for it all: a rented house that was not really a house at all. No land of his own. He did not have the strength to hold a regular job as a hired man; a few days' plowing in late winter would put him out of commission for a week; a few days' raking hay in the midsummer sun would do the same. He could handle horses if anyone kept enough horses any more to need a man to care for them. He really had nothing left except the ability to paint little pictures that amused and pleased people and sometimes made them feel sentimental. Over the years people had urged him to take his painting more seriously. Now he had to; there was nothing else left to do.

He had a few dollars left after paying his debts with the money he received for the last two mares and the plow. He went to Brownwood and bought a supply of paints, water color paper and tiny brushes. He looked at a newspaper in the paint store. There had been a blizzard in the Plains. All traffic had stopped, families were snowbound and cattle were starving. He wasn't so bad off after all.

He went home and began to paint.

Ranney-Hand Cows

Star Wagon Yard

Chapter 26

ALL through the years Kelly had painted, but he had done it casually, as naturally as a man might whistle while his mind was on something else. As a youngster he had loved to paint pictures of cows and horses. Before ever going West for the first time he had made drawings of how he imagined the West to be. Returning from his first trip to the West he had painted little pictures of men on horseback, broncos and working horses, trying to recapture for his friends some of the magic of the country. In the hard, poverty-ridden later years he painted pleasant scenes to send to his family and friends at Christmastime. He frequently illustrated his letters with tiny sketches in the margins. He entertained school children, his daughter's friends, by sketching in their notebooks, illustrating what he had told them about working as a cowboy and breaking horses, of riding a horse at a full run for a quarter-mile match race and driving a trotting horse on a fast track. Sometimes he had painted to take his mind off his troubles: during the worst of the dust storms in the Plains he had sat at night, his face swathed in damp cloths, and by the light of a gasoline lamp had drawn a whole series of sketches illustrating his beloved Pickwick Papers. In Blanket he had made pictures for friends, pictures of horses and horsemen, little snow scenes that he remembered from Michigan, Wyoming and Ohio. There was little else that he could give them as a mark of his friendship.

Kelly changed from part-time painter to full-time painter with an air of resignation rather than high resolve. There was no glowing conviction, no aching desire for expression of a personal vision. It was just that there was nothing left to do. Fortunately, it gave him great pleasure.

Inevitably, he remembered the days of his childhood, the days at his grandfather's place in Ohio. Someplace he had come across an old county atlas that described in detail the farms of the more prosperous citizens of Crawford County, Ohio. He studied the descriptions and remembered the farms themselves, or farms like them. He began a series of Ohio farm scenes: prim two-story white houses, stout red bank barns, orderly fields and orchards, men driving pigs to market or herding cows into the lot for milking, and always horses—trim, long-necked saddle and carriage horses and thick-flanked using horses. The Monnett farm, the Swisher farm, the John Ross farm. He took liberties with the houses as he remembered them, adding an ell here, a summer kitchen there; he enlarged the barns and moved them around at will; and he invented people and animals.

He searched his memory for scenes that he remembered: the look of teams plowing a field, seen from the rise of Salt Mountain, with the oaks russet and the sumacs rust-colored at the borders of the fields; the little tight stone houses nestled in the green hills below the Llano River; a blacksmith shop, stout work horses waiting patiently to be shod, the smith busily at work, men killing time with easy companionship.

Again and again he turned to the Bible as a catalyst to call up images in his own mind. He would read in the book of Isaiah: "And my people shall dwell in a peaceable habitation, and in sure dwellings and in quiet resting places. . . . Blessed are ye that sow beside all waters, that send forth thither the feet of the ox and the ass."

It had been many, many years since he had known anything of peaceable habitations or dwelling places. But the golden words swam in his head, and, working slowly as he always did, he began a picture that to his way of thinking bore them out: first the blue sky, then the purple-gray hills and the tiny faraway houses and the steeple of a church; a rolling landscape with a clear stream coursing through pleasant pastures, the trees in thick midsummer leaf; red cows grazing, a truculent white bull nearby. And farmers plowing their stubble fields, two teams—one of four mules, red, white, black and gray-blue; the other a team of four horses, sorrel, white, chestnut and black; the two plows turning up the tawny earth and leaving it rich and dark. The houses were sturdy, built of stone, with outside stairways, and on the porch of one a young farm hand gesturing and telling a tale to the farmer's daughter.

And again he would read: "Thou waterest the ridges thereof abundantly: thou settest the furrows thereof: thou makest it soft with showers: thou blessest the springing thereof. Thou crownest the year with thy goodness; and thy paths drop fatness. They drop upon the pastures of the wilderness: and the little hills rejoice on every side. The pastures are clothed with flocks; the valleys also are covered over with corn; they shout for joy, they also sing." And Kelly would think how sometimes in Texas there would be a green year, when the rains of spring continue into summer, when the springs and creeks run full through the hottest days, and the fields, instead of dry and yellow in the midsummer sun, are still lush and richly green. The little hills did, indeed, rejoice, and the pastures did shout for joy. And he would paint the green, sweeping hills, dotted with tiny sheep, and the geometrical cornfields in the valleys between and below.

The pictures began to accumulate. The problem of selling them had never occurred to him. He had always given them away before. He did not want to show them to his friends for fear they would, out of charity, offer to buy them; he would rather give them away than suffer that. He could not take them to the feed store or the market as he might a load of grain or a can of cream or a crate of eggs.

He began writing letters to artists whose names he knew, and to directors of museums and schools of art. He would tell them something of himself and the kind of painting he was trying to do: he was a farm hand who was doing some painting between crops. He gave no hint of his desperation, no hint that this was the only way left to him to make a living. All his life, he would explain, he had drawn memory pictures. As a child in upper Michigan, a cold and dismal country, he had remembered visits to his grandparents in Ohio and had tried to re-create the pleasant scenes that he had known, shutting out the present. It was a habit that had stayed with him all his life, recalling and painting the good things that he had known: fat cattle and sheep and hogs; fast horses and race meets in the summer; county fairs in the fall with the golden piles of grain and baskets of fruit and mounds of pumpkins; farm bakehouses with loaves of bread perfuming the air; smokehouses with great chains of sausage hanging in the shadows; springhouses with beaded brown bottles of homemade beer and stone crocks of pale yellow butter, bowls of clabber and great jugs of milk and heavy cream; the dusty excitement of riding a pitching horse and the deep, happy calm of a man plowing his own land with a thick-rumped team of mules; the freedom of riding for the ridge with all of one's worldly goods carried by a pack horse, and the great contentment of a man raking and stacking prairie hay in his own fields. It was a pleasure to recall these things from the past and paint them; perhaps they might give pleasure to those who were less fortunate than he.

Leafing through the stacks of old magazines that friends saved for him, he found some reproductions of paintings by Doris Lee. The simplicity of Miss Lee's paintings appealed to him. She had great skill and knowledge, but she took homely subjects, as he did, and painted them without fussiness but with, instead, love and respect. He composed a letter to Miss Lee and, unlike the others, this one brought a response. She invited him to send some of his pictures for her to see. Kelly shipped off a sheaf of seven water colors. In time back came an encouraging letter from Miss Lee with the suggestion that he might like to try his hand at oils, and also that he might well try to paint larger pictures. And, most encouraging of all, there was a check for one hundred dollars: a friend of Miss Lee's had seen the seven water colors, admired them and offered the enclosed check in payment. Kelly was delighted. He paid off some debts, had new soles and heels put on his boots and bought ten dollars' worth of canvas boards and oil paints.

The transition from water colors to oils gave him no particular trouble. Oils worked more slowly, but then Kelly worked slowly with water colors, and the result, in oil, had a strength and definition the water colors lacked. He continued to use the tiny brushes he had used for water colors, continued to paint his figures small, almost microscopic in some cases. He was delighted to find that with oil paints he could paint a roan horse—something that had been next to impossible, to his way of thinking, with water colors. He did not use a palette, but continued to use a compartmented water-color slant to mix his oils. He did not use an easel but worked flat on a table top. He found an old baby bed in the barn and converted it into a painting table with a flat surface, and sat on a high bench to work at it.

When he had three oils completed and varnished he was eager to ship them off. But they did not dry as rapidly as water colors. He covered them with wax-paper bread wrappers and took them into Brownwood and went to Howard Payne College.

Charles Stewart, head of the college art department, was the son and grandson of a Blanket ranching family that Kelly knew. Kelly appeared in the door of Charles Stewart's classroom and said abruptly, "Are you the Stewart boy that don't like cows and horses and is a painter instead?" Stewart admitted that he was. Kelly introduced himself and said he needed advice on how oil paintings should be wrapped for shipping.

Stewart looked at the paintings and was amazed. Kelly was obviously an untrained painter, and by most of the usual measurements he was a "primitive": he painted from memory; his approach was simple and direct; there was a natural feeling for design. But he was unlike most primitives. There was both linear and atmospheric perspective in his paintings. The figures of people and animals were in the round, not flat like paper cutouts. There was a dry, good-natured humor to the scenes, and with it a warm, unmistakable affection for both landscape and characters.

He helped Kelly prepare the paintings for shipment. Later, when they came back unsold, he arranged for them to be shown in a local paint and art supply store and

136

they were purchased by Brownwood people. Kelly was not getting rich but he was becoming well known locally and appreciated. Old farmers and ranchers began stopping by Kelly's house to see what he was painting. Almost without exception they were men who had considered art—if they considered it at all—as something that showed up on calendars. Yet they were impressed, seemed to know that what Kelly was doing was different, was far better. His horses were the way horses really were, not prettified. So were his mules and his working men. One old cowman stared grimly at a snow scene Kelly was painting, one row of snow-covered hills after another. "You can see clear to hell and gone back in those hills, Kelly," he said, "and the farther you go the colder it gets. What's it like to be an artist?"

"I'm not an artist," Kelly would say, "I'm just a horseman, an old stud and jack man, that likes to paint. By next year if I can get a little ahead, I mean to get a job handling horses again and I'll just paint in whatever spare time I may have. And after that I want to get me a farm again."

Charles Stewart loaned him art books, and Kelly pored over them at night or when his eyes were too tired for painting. He quickly chose his favorites: Pieter Brueghel the elder ("He liked to paint the simple, common crib-run of folks as I do") and George Innes ("His 'Peace and Plenty' is, to my mind, the most beautiful of all paintings").

"The more one looks at the work of fine old artists, the sorrier modern efforts seem. I often forget, though, that this young generation does not have the memories of beautiful scenes, either, that us old-timers have. No wonder they crave to see 'Westerns.' I often feel sorry for the kids. I was just lucky."

Stewart also presented Kelly to an auditorium full of students at Brownwood, introducing him as a natural painter who lived and worked among them, and compared his work with that of Brueghel.

"I'm really getting to be a tough, old soandso, the things I can take," Kelly wrote in a letter. "Can you imagine me, *cold sober*, sitting up there on a stage with a whole hall full of kids and teachers? I couldn't have done it, only through the love of Charles, who did the talking, and brother, is he a good talker! Before he got through I really thought I was Pieter Brueghel and not just old Redneck Kelly. Of course I had the moral backing of Jess and Maurine [Mrs. Charles] Stewart, sitting down there in the front row where I didn't even dare to look. The superintendent, a fine Irish-mugged young man, and two ladies, not hard to take, sat by me on the platform. Maurine held my hat, else I probably would have eaten it up. I like to talk to people if I can mill around with them, but it is hard to sit up front, cocked up there like a rat on a rafter. Afterward we went to the Postoffice Café and had ham hock and navy beans and I felt better."

The Brownwood and Fort Worth papers did feature stories on the area's newest celebrity, and more and more visitors found their way to the made-over chicken house. Some were painters of sorts who, impressed by the recognition that Kelly suddenly was receiving, sought his advice and criticism.

"I always give them nothing but good news. I am not a critic. I am a bearer of good tidings. There's enough grief in the world already without my adding to it. Anyhow, people that paint are blessed, and most of them are good company, too. They ask about my technique. Hell, if I got a technique I don't know where it is or what it is. I know there's plenty things I got no technique for. Like the colors in desert country. And the silvery mirages we used to see in the Plains; they were very beautiful shining above the dust. And the way the light has gold in it some days, especially along in the afternoon."

Some of the visitors were able to buy paintings and did not, and others genuinely wanted to and could not—and on occasion Kelly, who was poorer than any of them—would press paintings on them as gifts.

"There's so many poor people that love paintings and deserve them at poor people's prices. I guess I get most enjoyment out of other folks' pleasure."

Despite the agreeable distraction of a steady stream of callers, Kelly drove ahead with his painting, encouraged by the fact that for the first time in many years he was making a little money, thirty dollars here, fifty there. One enthusiast, Lexie Dean Robertson, of the nearby town of Rising Star, an amiable writer with a wide acquaintance around the state, bought one Kelly painting and borrowed three more unsold ones to send to Jerry Bywaters, director of the Dallas Museum of Fine Arts. Bywaters, an able artist himself and a critic with a strong feeling for regional art, promptly sold them to Dallas collectors and drove down to see Kelly. Would Kelly be interested in a one-man show at the Dallas Museum?

With his eyes squinted in a useless effort to hide the tears, Kelly said he would be. But, he cautioned, it would take some time to have enough paintings to make any kind of show; maybe another year. Working as slowly as he did and with time off for sick spells, he couldn't average much more than one painting a month. But he could do it; he had all the paintings right here—and he tapped his head; all he had to do was get them down on canvas.

It took more than a year for the one-man show to be organized. Thirty-seven paintings were assembled, six of them that Kelly had completed only recently and which were still unsold, and they were sold within the first hour of the exhibition. Attendance broke all records for a one-man show at the Dallas Museum. New York and Boston galleries wrote that they would like to represent him and show his paintings, and orders for pictures began to come from all parts of the country.

Chapter 27

SUCCESS brought certain adjustments in Kelly's life and way of living, but they were modest ones.

He moved to another house. It was, he said with characteristic warmth, "one of the loveliest old places around here." The rent was seven dollars and a half per month and it was an improvement over the old place in several respects. Although it, too, was without electricity or running water, was somewhat ramshackle—the stone chimney leaned drunkenly away from the house at a ten-degree angle, it was a little larger, more weatherproof and had never been inhabited by chickens. But most important, to Kelly, the rental of the house carried with it the right to a little fenced pasture in the rear. A man could graze a horse here, could keep up a horse if he had some cash coming in to buy feed during the winter months.

He had been without a horse too long. He had gone regularly to the bimonthly sales in Brownwood and stared sadly at the horses that were, for the most part, being sold to manufacturers of soap and dog food. Some were old and decrepit, used up; but many were there only because they were unneeded and unwanted, and this, for Kelly, was a desolate thought. He had spent more and more time with those of his friends who kept horses and had stated, repeatedly, that a man didn't have to *own* horses in order to admire and enjoy them.

Now, having money ahead and a place with a pasture, he bought a horse. He found an eight-year-old mare that pleased him. She had the head and neck of a thoroughbred and the sturdy back, flanks and legs of a quarter horse. She was capable of great bursts of speed over short distances, was nimble and quick-turning and might have been valuable as a working horse on a ranch, except that she was, for some reason, afraid of ropes. This was all right with Kelly, who said that "me and lariat ropes made peace a long time ago." And it brought the mare's price down within his reach.

He cleaned the old saddle and built a makeshift stall for the mare out of scrap lumber. Each morning he would carefully curry and brush her, saddle up and ride the quarter mile into the center of Blanket, check for mail, exchange greetings with anyone hanging round Allen's drugstore and Dabney's gasoline station.

Kelly's deep feeling about horses was well known in these circles. They joked about the way he had described an uncommonly good-looking schoolteacher who had come to admire his paintings: "As neat and pretty as a fresh-sheared mare mule." When old Doc Yantis was ill and Kelly had told Mrs. Yantis, "You take as good care of Doc as I would a good stud horse."

Somehow, having a horse of his own again had restored him to a position of dignity, prosperity and well-being. He recognized the fact that the little money he had coming in now hardly warranted keeping a horse that he didn't need for work, but he found justification for it.

"These good people have been encouraging me about my painting and they want me to keep on with it. I can't let them down. I've got to keep fit and keep painting, and the only way I can keep fit is riding a horse. The way I paint, I work from memory and out of thin air. I find I have to mill around some to keep from getting keyed up too high. Walking doesn't relax me any, but riding or even just fooling around with the mare does. I want to ride a horse as long as I can, and when I can't ride any more I want to sit by the window and have my mare tied outside where I can watch her. They don't talk back or complain or raise hell—they just repay you for kind treatment with cheerful service.

"I have yet to sit behind the wheel of a car and have the feeling that I could rise and fly, as I do on a horse, or that I can sit and look and let the horse think for me. You can turn a horse in at any gate or field, ride up the rows of crops— he will follow up the middle, letting you look all over at your leisure. If you are in a pasture looking for other horses, give him his head and he will take you to them, or to cattle. You are free to gaze everywhere, smell all the sweet scents and the rare ones, possum grape blooms in the timber, little baby breath flowers in the pasture, and corn tassels during those few days while the pollen hangs. Or he will carry you to the top of a ridge where you can survey the world in peace, see the rooftops and the pastures and the fields, see who is plowing and whether his furrows are straight or sorry, and it's easy to think how lovely the country was when only the Indians were here."

Whenever there was an audience Kelly would speak at length on the qualities of Babe, the mare, and of other horses he had owned and known.

"This mare I've got, she's fast as a striped ass monkey, and when I get a little ahead with my work I aim to make some money with her in match races. I let her out, now and then, just let her dust out on that caliche road that runs by our place, and she can really go. I've always liked mares to ride. I'm like the Arabs that way. Back in the old days in the West they wouldn't have anything but geldings in a re-muda; they thought mares and studs were only good for breeding. Well, I disagree with them. Mares are good to ride and work and so are stallions if you know how to handle them. Any horse colts I ever had I either left entire or traded them for fillies or for another stud, and let the buyer cut them if he wanted to, that was his business. As for the squealing and neighing, I'm like the man that runs that café in Brownwood and tells his customers to use plenty of sugar in their coffee and stir like hell, he doesn't mind the noise. They don't bother me; I like it. And I don't like eunuchs to ride; I want a *horse* and I'm man enough to ride one. And they aren't bad to handle if you know how to do it.

"Old Job, in the Bible, says something about the horse saying 'Ha, ha among the trumpets and he smelleth the battle afar off.' I think a good stud may say that when he sees or smells the girls, but if he's at home or you're in the saddle he just says, 'Hello, boss.' Back in the thirties in the High Plains I had a wonderful black stallion named Chief. He was blind in one eye and had a broken ear, but he was much horse and good to handle. I used to like to ride him over into a ten-section pasture that was still in grass and about the only green there was in that country. It was the old Laguna Grande pasture of the XIT. One day I rode Chief over there and there was one of the noblest sights I ever saw: a herd of mares that had been trailed down from Colorado, just as pretty as a picture. Of course old Chief bugled, but I rode him over toward the herd slowly, and he behaved very well. We rode around the herd, just looking, and those sleek little range mares just stood there, filled with curiosity, heads up, ears pricked forward, eyes bright and nostrils fluttering, ready to wheel and run in an instant, but old Chief didn't make a false move and after a while I rode slowly away and they were still just standing there.

"Later on I traded for two mares out of that herd. One was a little gray mare, almost white, that made a perfect mount for my daughter, Martha. And the other was a black-maned little dapple blue-gray bunch of dynamite that I called Dinkey. I believed she was the fastest thing to run and turn stock on that I ever rode. She could sort of read the minds of cows.

"Lots of people will say that a horse doesn't think or reason. They just don't know. Once when I had a filly colt to wean, back in Arkansas, I put her down off to pasture where she took up with a calf. I was working mules. The calf and the filly ran in a cotton field—there was grass all around the edge of the field, and there was a wild plum thicket for shade. Evenings my wife would call the calf to feed and the filly would come right along. One evening she called and the filly came along— the calf stayed behind, grazing on something. The filly just looked at my wife, and my wife kept on calling the calf. The filly wheeled around, ran back to the field and started nipping the calf on the rump and they galloped up through the cottonfield together, scattering blooms and bolls every which way.

"You ride a good horse out among the cows in the evening and he'll pick out those that are being milked and turn them toward the house, leaving the dry cows alone. I've done that lots of times, just leaving the reins loose and letting the horse do the work. One white mare I had was always in a hurry, and she would really nip the cows if I wasn't careful. She was anxious, always, and a *little* rough on cows.

"Once a good mare of mine died with acute colic, in spite of everything I did to help her. She left a mule colt, two days old. It was very sad. He walked up to where his mother lay, found the fountain dry, folded his legs and lay down by her, chin on the ground. I fixed him warm cow's milk, diluted with water and some lime water and sugar, and my wife fed him with a nursing bottle every couple of hours. Then he took to drinking milk from a pan and got so lively my wife was afraid to come to the lot unless he was penned: he would wring his tail and run up and down the fence yonking to her every time he saw her and would just climb all over her. Then I let him follow me in the field. He used to walk up behind me and stick his head under my arm, and if I wouldn't let him do that he would pull my shirt-tail out. I traded him at six months for a good mare, but I wish now that I'd kept him and trained him for a trick mule. I believe I could have taught him to do every-thing but read and write. A man makes mistakes like that.

"Once I traded for a new stud. He was seven years old and had been kept out with a bunch of mares, just for breeding. He was halter-broke, just to lead, that's all, not to work or ride. He was half Morgan and had that beautiful dark bay Morgan color. When I break strange horses I like to leave them in the corral a while and just go ahead working around them. He soon got right chummy with me. One drizzly day I was repairing some harness, working under the shelter of the long horse shed, and he was the only horse in the lot. He stood right over me, breathing down my neck. I happened to think I was working in his stall, so I moved my work over to another stall. But he came right after me, stood over me, breathing down my neck again. He just wanted to stand by me; it gave me a feeling of brotherhood. I harnessed him with a broke mare and drove them about. He hopped around some, but not too much, and the next day I harnessed him in a six-horse team and he worked perfectly. There was nothing in the work line he couldn't do well. I even broke him to ride, and he had a very pleasant running walk, nodding his head and ears. In hot weather I often fed him under a big live-oak tree where it was cool. The feedbox sat on the ground and it was made of heavy two-inch stuff. When his feed was about gone he would take one end of the feedbox in his teeth, raise it off the ground so that the feed would all roll to the other end where he could get at it easily. That's what I call reasoning, and people say that horses can't think just haven't been around the right horses. I kept that old stud as long as I worked horses and I wish I still had him. He sired many fine colts and gave me much pleasure."

Kelly's friends at the drugstore and filling station liked his tales and listened to them appreciatively, although few, if any, of them shared his deep feeling about horses. A horse was a handy tool—at times an indispensable one—but a pickup truck was even handier. Many of them actually rode their pastures and their fences in a pickup truck; if the location made a truck unfeasible they would haul the horse in a trailer and saddle up when they got there. And among themselves they joked about the hours Kelly spent brushing and currying his mare—and talking to her.

B. J. Stevens was one of the few that came close to feeling as Kelly did. He, too, loved horses, and got much pleasure from simply being around them. But he was, in addition, a somewhat more practical hippophile than Kelly, who, often as not, fell in love with a horse at sight. He chose his stallions and mares with a knowing eye toward the market for their colts. He roved far and wide, taking in horse sales, avoiding those where the discards were merely going to the soap or dogfood factory and making those where the well-heeled horse fanciers, the dudes, would appear. He seldom went to a sale without carrying along a horse in the trailer behind his pickup, ready to sell if someone would meet his price, ready to trade if it could be done advantageously, but never pushing either sale or trade, always waiting for the buyer or trader to take the initiative. He did very well at it, and Kelly admired him greatly, not only for his horsemanship but also for the business acumen which Kelly had always lacked in his horse trading.

B. J. had a good sorrel stallion, a registered horse that came from the King Ranch quarter-horse stock. His registered name was Coon Dog, but B. J. and Kelly between them never called him anything but Old Red. He was a powerful but gentle horse with a remarkable record for getting handsome, strong colts. Kelly fell in love with him and lamented that B. J. didn't keep him brushed and curried and sleek as he himself would have done. He would like, he said, to breed Old Red to his mare, Babe. If Kelly cleaned up Old Red, kept him and fed him, got him clean and handsome again, would B. J. let him keep the stallion for a while in the hope of getting one of his colts? B. J. agreed.

Delighted, Kelly took Old Red home, put him with the mare, fed him by hand, spent hours working over him with a curry comb and brush until his coat shone like a newly minted penny. The mare took Old Red and Kelly was happy as a child with Christmas coming. When he rode Babe into town later than usual, his friends at the drugstore and filling station asked him where he'd been.

"Talking to Old Red," said Kelly.

"Red who?"

"Old Coon Dog. B. J. Steven's stud. I'm keeping him for B. J. Going to get one of his colts, and then watch out, I'll really have me a horse."

"Talking to a stud horse?"

"Why, sure. Old Red's a better conversationalist than half the folks in Blanket."

Kelly might have kept Old Red on and on, but he became sick. Jessie Kelly was nervous around a stallion, as most women are, and didn't like to get near him, so while Kelly was ill B. J. had to come and take the stallion away again. Kelly missed seeing the big red horse in the little pasture, but he was comforted by the knowledge that he would, one day, have a colt that, God willing, would have the best qualities of both Babe and Old Red.

"Babe has two months yet to go. She's still lively and fast and wants to run, and I still ride her a little. Not too much belly; she's deep through the flanks anyhow, and it doesn't show. But great activity on the inside; I never saw a colt flop around so much. I see a race horse coming. About the time the oats green she'll have a wobbly-legged filly, I hope. It will keep me more around home for a while.

A little colt can find more damn ways to hang up its long legs. But we'll be at the Fredericksburg races in the summer of '53. Watch for us and put your money where it will do you some good."

Babe foaled her colt on February 16, 1951. There was snow on the ground. Kelly had watched the mare from the kitchen window. He ran out, got the newborn colt and hurried it into the shed where he rubbed its damp coat with a gunny sack and bedded it down in fresh straw that he had already prepared. It was a horse colt, the same copper sorrel color as his sire, and Kelly, although he had hoped for a filly, was overjoyed. This might be the horse of his life.

He spent hours with the colt, fondling and petting him as he would a puppy. Watching the colt's awkward gamboling in the yard, he decided he did, indeed, have the makings of a race horse: the colt would break into a full run from a standing start. He followed Kelly around, nuzzling him and, as his strength grew, rearing up and putting his forefeet on Kelly's shoulders. Jessie Kelly reminded him again and again that he should get to his painting, and Kelly agreed absently that he should, but went right on playing with the colt. The only painting he did was in a series of birth announcements that he made up for a few friends. In one corner of the little cards he drew and colored a picture of a lively, long-legged colt of unmistakable maleness; in the opposite corner a foaming shell of beer, with the advice: "Drink up!"

Feb. 16, 1951 A.D.
Red Hot-Bojangles.
Sire—King Ranch Coon Dog (Old Red).
Dam—Kelly's Babe.
Assisting—Conception & reception—yours truly—
    (and here a tiny arrow indicated an almost microscopic self-portrait, red-faced
    and big-nosed with a battered hat held in the air in salute. Then, finally:)
Visitors plenty & *welcome*.

Kelly predicted that Red Hot-Bojangles, or Little Red, as he called him, would be cleaning up at country tracks in a few years, and offered to take bets on it. He broke the colt to a halter but it was seldom necessary to use it; the colt followed at his heels wherever he went and would have followed him on his daily visits to the drugstore and filling station if Kelly had not shut him in the yard.

Kelly could talk of little else. On a trip to a horse sale in Comanche with B. J.

Stevens, Kelly found himself in the conversation with a horse buyer from north Texas, and began describing the wonders of his colt. The horse buyer said he'd been looking for a good horse colt and would like to see Kelly's. Kelly was delighted to show off the colt. The stranger followed B. J. and Kelly back to Blanket and agreed that this was, certainly, a fine colt. What would Kelly take for him?

B. J. knew that Kelly did not want to sell the colt; he also knew that a colt such as this one should bring $225.

Selling the colt was the farthest thing from Kelly's mind. But for some reason that he could never explain to himself afterward, he decided to name a price which he was sure would end the conversation, a price so far above anything he had ever before received for a colt that it would appear ridiculous.

"Seventy-five dollars," he said.

The man reached in his pocket, pulled out a checkbook, quickly filled out a check and handed it to Kelly.

Kelly was stunned. He protested: the colt wasn't weaned yet; it was too early; why didn't the man come back in six months and they could talk about a deal then. The stranger shook his head. Kelly had named his price and it had been met; the colt was old enough to be weaned and he would attend to it. A truck would come to pick up the colt the next day. Once gelded, the colt would make a fine saddle horse.

Kelly knew that he could tear up the check and stop the transaction. But he also feared that word would get around that he, Kelly, who thought of himself as a horseman, was a man who backed out of horse deals. This was just something a horseman didn't do. When the truck came the next day he told the driver where the colt could be found; he stayed at his painting table, staring at a canvas on which he had completed only the blue sky.

B. J. Stevens sympathized with him and promised that when the time came they would again breed Babe to Old Red.

Kelly returned to his painting and tried to shut out any thought of Little Red and what had happened to him.

One Sunday morning in October, 1952, he had saddled Babe, preparatory to taking a ride along some of the back roads where the foliage might be turning. He left her in the yard and went off to attend to some chores. When he returned the mare was gone. He walked up the caliche road until he found her. She was consorting with a big black horse that a neighbor had recently acquired, an ugly hammer-headed, gaunt-framed animal that had been destined to be a gelding but had somehow ended up a ridgeling. The castration operation had been inadequate and the beast was neither stallion nor gelding. Kelly had known ridgelings in the past; they were generally ill-tempered, hard to work with. Their only useful purpose was to tease mares and get them in an emotional state conducive to breeding to a selected stud. Sometimes, Kelly knew, a ridgeling would get a colt, despite his biological handicap. And he wondered if this ugly creature had accomplished anything with Babe.

At the first opportunity Kelly took Babe back to B. J. Stevens' stallion, Old Red, and tied her in the corral. The handsome red horse picked up his ears and trotted over to the mare with interest—and just as suddenly lost his interest and returned to his feedbox.

"Kelly, that mare's been bred," said B. J. "That's why Red won't have anything to do with her."

"Good God, I hope not," said Kelly.

They tried again a week later. Again Old Red showed no interest.

"Kelly, there's no use," said B. J. "Us old men sometimes fool ourselves. Old horses never do. That mare's in foal."

Kelly told him about the encounter with the ridgeling.

"I'd hoped that this time I would get a colt that I could keep for the rest of my life," he said.

Eleven months later Babe dropped a horse colt—an ugly blocky creature. Kelly gave him away at the first opportunity and comforted himself with the thought that he had, in his lifetime, had some very fine horses.

Blacksmith and Wagon Shop

Sunday Morning

Chapter 28

ALL his life Kelly wanted to be someplace else. As a boy in school he had yearned to be out plowing the fields. As a machinist's apprentice he dreamed of being a cowboy in the West. He fancied himself as a rancher in Wyoming, a homesteader in Nebraska, a farmer in Missouri, a cotton-grower in Arkansas, a stock farmer in Texas. In the High Plains he wanted to be anyplace in preference to where he was, but preferably in a place where men still farmed with animals, where there might be water, woods and hills. He never ceased dreaming of places he had not seen, and when he began painting he created a country of his own, a country that had bits and pieces of Pennsylvania and Ohio, Texas and Arizona, Nebraska and Arkansas, all with a strong flavor of the nineteenth century when men lived with more dignity and humor, less desperation and more joy.

The world he painted was one of tidy houses made of clapboard or native stone; orderly fences, gracious trees and sweeping vistas of hills and valleys, well-tilled fields and green pastures, and, always, happy people.

One of his neighbors in Blanket stopped to watch him at work on one of his early paintings.

"Why, Kelly," he said, "that looks just like Fredericksburg, where my sister lives."

Kelly had often heard of Fredericksburg. His brother Quill had been there once and had described it in loving detail: the stone houses, the woods and rivers, the pleasant, solid, German-speaking people who went about their business in seemly fashion. Kelly had read more about it. It was in the heart of the hill country of southwest Texas, high in the Edwards Plateau, a region bounded on the east by the Balcones fault and on the west by wide, empty plains. It was a country that charmed and surprised newcomers, unlike anything they had been led to expect in Texas: tumbled hills and fertile valleys along the spring-fed rivers; parklike woods and dense thickets where there were deer and wild turkey. It had been settled a century earlier by serious-minded German immigrants. They had named their town for Frederick the Great of Prussia, had made a treaty with the Comanches, and, hating slavery, had been on the outs with their Anglo-American neighbors during the Civil War. This difference in opinion plus the natural isolation of the area had helped make them self-sufficient. They had kept to themselves, developing their own economy, preserving the old language and the old ways of life.

When his paintings began to sell Kelly took a trip to Fredericksburg. He rode hunched forward in his seat while the bus raced uphill and down along the twisting highway. His tin suitcase rested on the floor between his boots. The soiled gray-white hat was pushed back on his head. His small, quick eyes darted from one side of the road to the other with the excitement of a child. Settlements flashed by. The little river sometimes ran along the road, first on one side, then the other, following its course over beds of gravel and limestone shelves, flowing clear and green with the spring water that trickled down from the hills and across the pastures. Dry rock walls, stones cleared from the land and carefully balanced in neat files, bordered the road. Between the rock walls and the highway were jungles of roadside asters, the lavender flowers barely visible in the gray-green foliage, strident clumps of fire-wheel, stately white Mexican poppies and ashen clusters of senisa, dead-seeming now in the summer heat. Sycamores, willows and pecans bordered the river, with here and there a cypress, tall and remote. Back in the pastures clumps of liveoak cast umber shadows in which cattle stood, flicking flies with their tails. A buzzard picked and tore at the flattened carcass of a raccoon on the hot pavement, and as the bus rumbled across a stone bridge a dozen painted turtles slipped into the water from a mossy log. A mockingbird and a blue jay quarreled noisily over a mustang grape-vine. A field lark whistled sweetly, and from back in the hills came the tinkle of goat bells. The ranch land gave way to farming country, pastures gave way to small clean fields, rock walls to wire fences, the cedar posts close-set, the strands running taut and straight. Here was an orchard of gold and red peaches, a vineyard with fast-ripening grapes, a barnyard with fat pigs, a haystack, a great barn with the white-blazed face of a horse staring from a window.

The highway straightened and swept down into Fredericksburg. The bus rattled along a main street that was wide and clean and uncrowded, and came to a stop.

Kelly took a deep breath and thought that coming to this town, which he had never before seen in his life, somehow seemed like coming home after all the years of wandering. It was like Ohio and Pennsylvania all over again.

He climbed down from the bus and walked to the hotel, solid and old-fashioned with rocking chairs on the sidewalk in front, and as he walked along he looked at the people on the street, half expecting to find a familiar face. He asked for a small, cheap room at the hotel and was shown into room 107. There was an old walnut spool bed. It was like the bed in which he had been born. Lying on it he could look out in the rear courtyard, bounded by a stone wall, vine-covered and loud with bird songs.

He washed his hands and face in the lavatory, wet down and brushed his wiry hair, punched out the crown of his hat and walked out on the street. His bowed legs and booted feet were unaccustomed to walking on anything but turf and bare earth, and then not for any distance if he could help it. He had the horseman's scorn for walking. But he stumped on up the street, preoccupied with the beauty of the town, forgetting the discomfort of his feet.

The buildings, houses and stores alike, were old and staunchly built of limestone, cured and burnished to a mellow amber by the sun, wind and rain; the brushed joints of mortar formed a white web against the yellow of the stone. Tin roofs, like pewter, softly reflected the glare of the late afternoon sun. Between the houses elms and cedars shaded pleasant green lawns and tidy gardens bordered with pink brick and whitewashed stones. Some of the houses were large—the residences of town people, the merchants, the professional men. Scattered among them were the little "Sunday houses." These had been built many years ago when the roads were difficult and a farm family's journey to town was a vast undertaking. They would come to town on Saturday, do their trading and shopping, and stay in their own little house— a room or two downstairs, and an outside stairway leading to the attic where the children could sleep. In the evening the children might play their singing games—

Heinzelmaenchen hat kein Endchen,
Kann kein Endchen finden. . . .

And the parents might gather in the beer garden, listening and sometimes dancing to nostalgic music, talking softly and drinking their beer. On Sunday the whole family would go to services at the Vereins Kirche, the men entering by one door, the women another. Later the men would go to the weekly rifle shoot, the women to sew and talk together. Or the family might go to a songfest to join in the old German songs and hymns they had known from their fathers and their fathers' fathers. Then the long trek back to the farm or ranch, and five more days of hard labor.

Kelly walked all over the town: to the museum that occupied a replica of the church that was shaped like a coffee mill; to the fairgrounds, inside the town limits, with its half-mile track and the view of the rooftops and steeples. He stopped in a restaurant and had a meal of beer, hard-boiled eggs and potato salad made in the German way with bacon fat, vinegar and onions. He rested for a while in a rocking chair in front of the hotel, listening to the *Abendglocken* ring out the signal for men to stop their work, and, remembering how his grandmother had taught him and his brother to sing, in German, of the evening bells. Later he walked to one of the taverns, drank his beer slowly and watched the men playing dominoes and scat, talking to each other in German; he admired an old man with long white mustaches who sat in a corner, magnifying glass in hand, reading a German newspaper. He left and walked to an open-air dance pavilion where colored lights hung in the oak trees. Stout waitresses brought pitchers of beer to families sitting together, and portly couples waltzed with great dignity.

He was up early the next morning. He bought a cheap box camera at a drugstore, loaded it with film and made pictures of some of the wonderful little stone houses. It was strange, he thought. This was a place he had been painting without ever having seen it. The country looked the way he had always thought country should look, the way he had tried to make it look in his paintings. Things were neat, well ordered, seemingly unaffected by a frantic, twentieth-century world. It was the kind of world, he thought, that his grandparents had come from: the old world of Switzerland and Germany. The kind of world he had sensed as a child, but had never really found.

When the northbound bus pulled out Kelly took a seat in the rear so that he could look back on the lovely old town until it disappeared behind the hills. He slipped his boots off his aching feet and thought of the things that he wanted to paint: the stone houses, rearranged and grouped around a little plaza instead of in a line, as they were; the handsome old house with the portico and the iron grill-work; the vineyard and winery and the bottles of "Pride of Fredericksburg" wine; the tannery and the saddlemaker's shop; the old bakery with a loaf of bread painted on the window and the sign advising that pumpernickel was on hand, smelling as the old bakeries did, not like the new ones which made him think only of shaving soap; the water mill and the burying ground on Bear Mountain with the grave markers for the pioneers; the dance pavilion, the German band, the red-faced bartender cutting the heads from schooners of beer, the stout couples whirling gracefully on the floor.

He would, he thought, move to Fredericksburg, just as soon as he saved some money. It would not matter if he sold paintings or not. Back in the hills there were dude ranches that accommodated the people from Houston, Austin and San Antonio who liked to get into the cool uplands and ride horses. He could always make a living as a horse wrangler; it was better than raking and baling hay, building fences, carpentering. And in time he would have his own string of horses again, breed them, break and train them, possibly even race them. He'd like to run some quarter races on that track at Fredericksburg.

Chapter 29

IT was, for Kelly, the first of many trips to Fredericksburg. Whenever money came in for a painting, he would first settle his note at the bank (he borrowed against paintings to come just as he had once borrowed for seed to put in a crop), then pay the doctor and the drugstore, buy a present for his wife, pay for the constant repairs that were needed to keep his ancient car going, lay in a case of beer to store in the cool wellhouse, and if there was any money left, as he said, "to jingle," he would make another pilgrimage to the German-flavored town in the hills. He always tried to be there for the Gillespie County fair; any time was good, but this was the best. He would wander among the stables, talking casually with the horse owners and trainers. He would listen to the German band in the grandstand. With a cool bottle of beer in his hand, he would lean against the paddock fence and watch the races. Between races he would stare out across the gentle valley of Fredericksburg, taking pleasure in the sight of rooftops and steeples just visible above the thick green of the trees.

Nights he would wander from tavern to dance hall and back to tavern again, barely sipping his beer, enjoying the music, watching the stout, florid men, the buxom women and the red-cheeked children. In the taverns he would, at times, strike up a conversation, and the natives would laugh good-naturedly at the fragmentary German he remembered from his boyhood in Ohio. When a wedding supper was held in one of the halls he sat on the back step, beer in hand, staring at the starry sky and listening with pleasure to the clatter of people inside. Late at night he would lie on the spool bed in room 107 at the Nimitz Hotel, watching the starched white curtains stir in the night air, listening for the mockingbird that came to sing in the vines of the courtyard. In the morning he would rise and walk about the town, breathing the cool upland air, sensing the freshness of the gardens, wet with dew, stopping to look in the blacksmith shop where the forge was beginning to glow. He would walk to the track and watch the horses being exercised, and stomp his way back into town for a breakfast of spicy, old-fashioned sausage, coffee cake crumbling with cinnamon and butter and coffee with thick cream. He would return to the hotel, take off his boots (although Western boots were never made for a pedestrian, Kelly would not think of going about in public in anything but boots), put on house shoes and sit in a rocking chair on the sidewalk. Many of the people had come to know him by sight and smiled pleasantly when he said *"Guten Morgen"*; yet he could not honestly say that he had any friends in the town. They kept to themselves and ignored outsiders. He had made casual inquiries as to the availability of a farm to buy or rent, but had found nothing. Nobody here ever sold or rented their land. If land was sold it went to a kinsman or friend.

This did not bother Kelly. This was the way a solid, settled community was, and he did not resent their seeming indifference. And he carried the best of Fredericksburg in his head, anyway.

He still talked with friends of some day "getting a little ahead and moving to Fritztown." And he would say, "I'd sooner scratch a poor man's ass in Fredericksburg than own all of Coney Island," but he no longer believed it. Each time he came home, Blanket seemed better, his friends finer.

When a wealthy ranch family, impressed with the old man's paintings and charmed with him as a person, invited him to come and live on their place in the hill country, to look after the horses as little or as much as he wanted, and paint as much as he could, he declined for reasons that he could not easily explain to them. It was not that he had any degree of security where he was. His paintings were selling well, but the return was slight in relation to the amount of time he spent on them. And his production was always being cut off by bouts of illness.

It was not that he feared losing his independence; he might lose everything else but this he could never surrender, even if he should want to. It was just that some of the old restlessness was disappearing. The demanding curiosity that had driven him back and forth across the country, from ocean to desert, from mountains to plains, from prairies to backwoods, from swamps to tableland, was somehow lessening, dying. He found that he could look at a fine field without wanting to make a crop in it, could watch a pitching horse and have no desire to ride it, could admire a great stallion without wanting to own him.

On one of his trips to Dallas where, after his successful exhibition, he was the object of some lionization, he was entertained in a palatial house on White Rock Lake. His host was E. DeGolyer, the famed geophysicist, a man of both great wealth and intellect. The library alone was twice as large as any house Kelly had ever lived in, and there were books all the way to the ceiling—a lifetime of reading. Kelly appreciated the good taste and scholarship represented in the books and in the paintings and antiques that filled the house.

"You've got a mighty fine place here," he told DeGolyer at the end of the evening. "As grand as an old Spanish governor's palace. Noble. And a man could spend his life in that library and never miss anything. But, you know, I wouldn't trade with you."

He still, sometimes, spoke longingly of the little sixty-acre farm he would like to own, how he would plant and manage it, and of the fine horses he would like to raise and train. But he no longer mentioned these things with determination; his life was pleasant as it was.

Kelly's friends, noting his increased tranquillity, his diminishing impatience, concluded that this was the peace of old age. But they did this in private, not within Kelly's hearing. Kelly did not like to admit that he was getting old.

He revered elderly people. He often spoke admiringly of men in their nineties who still chopped wood and did some plowing; of women in their eighties who still could raise a fine garden, bake a rich pie, laugh at a joke and waltz gracefully.

"I notice," he would say, "that the captains of the great ocean liners aren't downy-cheeked boys. And the engineers that drive the fast trains—the railroads don't trust equipment like that to any but the old hands. And look at the really great horse trainers—you've got to be along in years to know as much as they know."

But he did not admit that he himself had reached old age.

When an optometrist urged him to wear bifocal glasses Kelly snorted, "Those are for old people," and ordered, instead, two pairs of glasses, one for painting and reading, another for distance vision. He maintained that he did not really need the latter since he saw "too damn much without any help."

When one of his best friends unwittingly described him, in conversation with a third person, as an "old gentleman," Kelly overheard it, and it almost destroyed the friendship.

In conversation with younger people he never conceded a difference in their ages. "You remember when McKinley was shot?" he would say. "Well, that was when

I was working for Lafayette Yeagley." Or: "You remember when 'Seeing Nelly Home' came out, when we were all singing it?" The Spanish-American War was as recent as the Korean conflict, and the truculence of Teddy Roosevelt was as fresh in his mind as the suavity of Franklin Delano Roosevelt—and he sometimes puzzled at the blank expressions in the faces of his visitors when they did not grasp this.

He grieved deeply over the death, first, of his much-loved younger brother, Quill, and then of his father. He was shaken by the death of Peter Files. They had been close friends and neighbors, both in Arkansas and the High Plains, had married sisters, and Pete was exactly two months older than Kelly. Kelly wrote to his sister: "He had lots of machinery, a car, a truck, four thousand bushels of wheat in the bin, three hundred acres of wheat, and thirty yearlings. He worked seven days a week, hot, cold, wet and dry. He worked too hard. You only pass through this world once, and I want to enjoy all the beauty there is; you don't do it buzzing down the road at sixty miles per hour."

He sometimes thought of his own death, frequently said he was not yet ready "to ride the pale horse . . . I only want to ride old Babe. I am better acquainted with her. I want to live to be a good *old* man."

He lost his teeth with no regret. One came out in a fight on the docks of Elizabeth, another when a mule had kicked him in the face in Nebraska. Several had been removed with the help of corn whisky and veterinary forceps. Finally he had only one lower incisor, which he kept because it was handy for drawing the string of a Bull Durham sack. When his friend B. J. Stevens had to go to a dentist Kelly went along, and to share his discomfort had his one remaining tooth drawn. This was a considerable mark of friendship, he told B. J., because "March-born people have teeth that are set like a donkey's."

He spurned dentures, but he was proud of the fact that he held his jaw in a state of suspension, lips closed, so that until he opened his mouth to speak, eat or drink people did not know he was toothless. Because he had many callers, many of them women, he was careful of his appearance. He still rubbed his face with Red Arrow liniment after a shave to stimulate the feeling of having *really* shaved. He shaved every day, and every day put on a fresh, blue work shirt. He spent much time in front of the mirror, combing and brushing the hair that had, he said, once been "a sort of blue roan color" but was now thickly flecked with gray. He joked about his long, bulbous nose, twice broken by fists and once by a horse's hoof, and about his small, close-set eyes: "You see anybody with possum eyes like mine, set on the bias, like, you can bet they're horse people and adventurous, too." He often spoke of how Quill had been big and handsome while he, Kelly, was undersized and ugly, but it was without resentment, and it did not detract from his vanity. He was mildly apologetic for his present cleanliness and neatness, and would assure friends that he had not always been so. "I used to always start the week clean on a Monday morning, and then get egg or sirup or catsup—or all three—on my shirt at breakfast, and all week long I kept adding dust, grease, oil, etc. By Saturday noon I looked and smelled like a real dirt farmer. I used to enjoy the compound odor of sweat, plug tobacco, horses, whisky and the hog lot. Hired men don't smell good any more."

He was in his glory on trips to Dallas when well-dressed, handsome women clustered around him, admiring his paintings and wanting to hear about his life and experiences. He frequently was a guest in their homes, but he was studiously correct in excusing himself, if, for any reason, the husband was called out of town. He would not willingly put temptation in anyone's way, even his own.

Besides, there were many simple, uncomplicated pleasures in his life. Perhaps the greatest was the nearness of his two grandsons, Harold and Clifford. They came to see him frequently, would ride the mare bareback around the yard with a halter, go hunting along the creek. They loved nature and were, in many ways, as he and his brother Quill had been. Kelly began putting the two of them, always together, in almost every painting he made. He thought he saw something of himself in each of them. Harold had his love of farm animals, and Clifford loved books and painting. Together they would watch the squirrels in the mulberry tree, the wren in the mailbox, and in the evening Kelly would tell them of antelope grazing among the cows in Wyoming, of the great snowstorms in Nebraska, of timber camps and shipwrecks in northern Michigan.

More and more people sent him books to read. He developed great enthusiasm for contemporary Texas writers, Tom Lea, Frank Dobie, George Sessions Perry, Sigman Byrd. When the University of Oklahoma Press brought out a new edition of *The Horses of the Conquest* by Robert Cunninghame Graham, the Dallas *News* book editor, Lon Tinkle, asked Kelly to review it. Kelly was well acquainted with the subject, having made a close study of the Maudsley translation of Bernal Diaz del Castillo. He agreed gladly, and wrote:

"Thanks be to Robert Cunninghame Graham, a noble *caballero* and may God rest him, who at the age of 78 wrote this book . . . not only for us horse idolators but for everyone who loves travel and adventure . . . [he writes] as one who worked, fought, rode and played with the hands who got the job done." Kelly retells, from Cunninghame Graham, the story of a missionary priest finding, years later, a stone idol of a horse, made by Indians with whom Cortez had left an ailing animal. The priest destroyed the stone figure. "The world," wrote Kelly, "would have been better off if the reverend father had had more Indian beer and less zeal in his belly."

Kelly liked to read stretched out on a chair pallet on his porch, his trousers hanging on nail nearby in case lady visitors might drive up. In the evening when it was cool he liked to lie, reading on his bed in the front room with a fire of Spanish oak and mesquite in the stone fireplace, crackling and burning clean.

His life, he thought, was very fine and full. There were few things that irritated him any more: blister bugs; the impossibility of getting a good beargrass hat for summer wear; and the johnnies-come-lately in the cattle business, the people who, knowing nothing of stock farming, had bought cattle just at the time he had had to sell all of his, and in so doing had become rich and arrogant on inflated beef prices. But then the blister bugs always went away; any kind of hat would keep the sun off a man's head; you could ignore the seven-day wonder cattlemen; and the only people that really seemed to need money were a man's creditors.

He was secretly aware that even his closest friends regarded him as somewhat strange. When he developed a case of mumps at the age of seventy he at first ignored them, with the inevitable result. He tried to paint sitting on the edge of the bed, and, finding this too uncomfortable, resorted to writing letters to friends.

"I would like to have a good laugh," he would write. "What I mean is, just fold up. I would like to go to an old-fashioned burlesque or minstrel show. No movies or radio wisecracks for me. I am feeling droopy.

"Well, the only people in the world that amount to a damn are the merry ones and the grateful ones. I'm glad that I'm fitted up like my friend *equus caballus* instead of like old Gus, the boar, who has them stuck on behind. That *would* be uncomfortable. I guess I'm lucky to be around, and very thankful for many things, besides that. I hope I outlive old Methuselah. This is a fine world. I like it. It grows on me.

"But my friends around here get somewhat wild-eyed in discussing my condition, as if to say, 'What will that crazy old bastard do next?'"

Chapter 30

WHILE he was laid up with the mumps Kelly gave up smoking, a habit of fifty-four years' standing.

"Now," he wrote, "I've quit coughing up all that dirt I picked up in the Plains. I have taken to chewing Beech Nut, a good scrap tobacco. Not that I care much for chewing. But I fill my head with that when I crave a smoke and it takes away the desire for it—and for damned near anything else. I sleep and breathe okay and do not cough at all. I arose this morning, put on my slippers and levis and walked out onto the gallery and pissed into the yard the way a man should. I am in good shape. One hundred forty pounds, hair blue, eyes red and rarin' to go. Full of Vitamin P— potato salad and beer. No telling, I may even be able—in time and with plenty ale— to accumulate a few concubines (self-supporting) and, what's more interesting at this point, sing bass again. Sing 'After the Ball is Over' to see the old stews weep in their beer, and then give them 'Only a Bird in a Gilded Cage' to knock them plumb off. Why, another fellow and I back in Arkansas used to sing bass against eight tenors and drown them out. I'd like to do that again—but then you don't find all the coons up one tree. I'll settle for whatever I can do, even if it's only beating a drum.

"I've had much pleasure from music in my life and I aim to have a lot more. The best music, of course, is the music of nature. The wonderful night songs of the mockingbird, sung over and over again, and better each time. The puzzling, lonely call of the whippoorwill. The crowing of roosters in a strange town at dawn, to be equaled only by the matins and vespers of the noble jackass. The nickering of mares and the grunt of pigs, all of these things are grand if your ear is tuned to them.

"I have always loved the old songs, the sweet songs and the solemn ones as well as the gay and lively: my grandmother teaching me '*Oh wie wohl ist mir am Abend*' and '*Ein' feste Burg*' when I was a little boy. And all the great old songs that Quill and I used to sing when we were young fellows in New Jersey, before we went West—'In the Good Old Summertime' and 'The Spanish Cavalier', 'Juanita' and 'Daisy Bell' and 'Seeing Nellie Home.' And the Mexican songs in Arizona, with all the yiping and yowping, and the lumberjacks up in Michigan singing about the jam on Gerry's rock, and the Irish on the railroad gang singing about Kevin Barry. Up in Nebraska they used to sing about 'when I was single my money did jingle, Oh, I wish I was single again,' and they even had a song about homesteading that ended up 'This noble Moses P. Kinkaid.' They were always making up words to go to the tune of old songs. They sang that one to the tune of 'Tannenbaum.' In the Dakotas they used to sing about it never raining and ending up 'till Gabriel blows his trumpet sound and says the rain's just gone around.' They sang that to the tune of 'Beulah Land,' and I don't think they came up to the original in either case; they are grand old songs. Some of the old-timers in Arkansas were still singing about the Bonnie Blue Flag, and everybody sang those sad old folk songs, songs about people getting poisoned and rosebushes growing out of their graves, things that had come straight down from the English. But what I liked best was the Negroes and the spirituals they sang at their meetings. And their street cries—the old man that sang about his cold chicken and hot weenies, and there were others that sang about fresh catfish right out of the river, and about strawberries, ripe and sweet, and even the junk man had a melodious cry that he used to sing out. Old Ab Green, the bullwhacker, had an odd little song he used to sing to his oxen when he hitched them up, but I could never make out the words or the tune either, he sang it so low, and I didn't like to ask him since it was a sort of private thing between him and the cattle.

"I don't really have many regrets about my life, misspent as it's been, but one thing I'm sorry for. When I was a boy in Scottdale they organized a boys' band. My brother and I both signed up, and they issued me a piccolo, and I just turned up my nose at it, thinking it was a sissy instrument. What I really wanted was a tuba, or something big and grand like that, so I passed up the one chance I had to really learn music. A boy is always passing up opportunities, and I've passed a lot of them, but that one I really regret.

"In Elizabeth a little German band used to come and play on the street corner, and my mother would put a few silver coins on the windowsill for them. And on the Jersey City ferryboat there used to be an Italian trio, two fiddles and an accordion. I would just ride that ferryboat back and forth and follow them around the decks while they played.

"I learned to play the French harp and I've played it in more places than I can remember, in bunkhouses and livery stables, in haystacks where I bedded down for the night, in freight cars, in railroad camps, in hobo jungles and even in hotel rooms when I was in a strange town and lonely. I learned to pick the guitar, and I got so I played harp and guitar at the same time, and many's the time in the High Plains that neighbors would get together and we would all play and sing together, 'On Christ the Solid Rock I Stand' and 'Sweet By and By' and 'Abide with Me,' and it always sort of took our minds off our troubles. I had rather sing than play— I can only play in the keys of C and G—but then dust and Durham fixed my voice so I can't do any more than croak.

"One thing I like about Fredericksburg is those Germans are a singing people. Before I ever went there I asked one old German if there was much music in Fredericksburg, and he said, 'Schure, everywhere iss choirs.' If ever I move down to Fredericksburg to stay, I know I don't have voice enough left to sing with them, but I'd like to join a German band and beat the drum for them, just for the joy of the beer and the dancing on a Saturday night. A little band, a quadrille, stout couples one-stepping, beer being unloaded and iced in kegs, and horses and mules eating sheaf oats in the lot; a few songs while the band is resting and taking on the suds; then the roll of drums and the 'oompah' of the big horn and the happy people dancing again."

Kelly's love of music formed his strongest tie with organized religion, an attachment which was, at once, both strong and flexible. Reared a Presbyterian, Kelly was joyfully indiscriminate in his attitude toward sects. It was enough, he thought, that people should wish to come together to pray and sing, and this, by itself, was good, no matter what they might specifically believe. All through his wandering years he made it a point to attend church services when and where he could. Arriving in a strange city, there were always three things that he did. If there was a Chinese restaurant, he had a double portion of chop suey. If there was a burlesque theater, he took in a show. And he went to church, or, rather, churches. He might attend an early morning Catholic mass, a Methodist Sunday school, a Presbyterian morning service and a Baptist evening prayer meeting. Singing hymns with these people made him seem less a stranger, less alone.

He was impervious to theological argument, sectarian differences and exegetical harangues and respected no denomination's monopoloy on righteousness and godliness. He knew his own Bible and interpreted it to his own satisfaction. His own very personal form of worship was transacted in the fields, under the trees and the sky. He believed in a hereafter, but it wasn't a place of saintly characters (whom he found rather dull for the most part). There would be all the goodhearted, laughing people he had ever known, as well as the preachers and teachers and Sunday school superintendents. "There will be plenty good bartenders, whores, horse traders and gamblers receive the crown for their good deeds, as well as ordinary sinners who are kindhearted and forgiving." And although he wasn't entirely sure of it he hoped he'd see again all the noble animals he had owned and loved—Old Bright, the notable cow that produced an unbroken line of lovely daughters, only to succumb to dust fever in the Plains, and Chief, the gentlemanly black stallion that died of eating grasshopper poison. "It's sad when a good horse dies. You've done all in your power for your friend and servant. You kneel, hand on his neck, you watch the four feet beat into a little trot. The big eyes glaze and the nostrils flutter with a soft nicker. You know your horse has a place to go, and sees it already. If you're lucky you'll go there too."

He took exception to all missionary efforts, and thought that the benighted tribes of Africa and Oceania had as much right to worship in their ways as he, Kelly, did in his. "I take a very smoky view of churches breaking in and proselytizing. Any religion is okay for people if they already have it. The Indians' green corn dance with their corn beer and potlatches was better, to my notion, than some of these hell-fire services I've been to. They thanked the Great Spirit very kindly and a good time was had by all."

In his late years in Blanket his churchgoing was a seasonal matter. During the winter months he stayed home; the churches were overheated and the short winter days allowed little enough time for painting. "I stay home and drink good German Lutheran beer and Roman Catholic vinous beverages, and listen to Methodist, Presbyterian, Baptist and Catholic services on the radio with my sock pointed at the open door of the stove."

In the summer he made up for it by attending at least twice each Sunday, morning and evening, dividing his attendance between the four congregations that the town of Blanket supported. "I have friends in all four churches, and go to all, since I don't want to be partial; and if I am in Brownwood on a Sunday I like to go to Catholic mass; Father Harrison is a fine little priest."

In the summer the churches held series of revival meetings, frequently with a visiting evangelist. One such revivalist was a man after Kelly's own heart: he kept a stud horse and a pack of coon hounds.

But Kelly took exception to most of them. "I have been to two revivals, Methodist and Church of Christ, and before that the Cumberland Presbyterian, and the week before I went to three revivals and one calf-roping. It gives me exercise to get out and go, and also it rests my eyes—I would only read at home. It is quite interesting to watch the motions of dressed-up ladies who find blister bugs. Those damned things. Job missed something! Sometimes the preaching is rather hard on me. You can almost hear the lost souls screaming and smell the brimstone—although sometimes it's those damned deodorants women use; I prefer for women to smell the way God intended. Most of the revival preachers shout too much, and I don't like to be hollered at. I've been going to one that's supposed to be a youth revival. There are no lost youths around Blanket that I know of. They are pretty good kids. So the preacher had slim pickings. I went to the Baptist revival last summer out of respect to the regular preacher, a very good man. But the last night was too much for me. The evangelist, the head-bobbing billy-goat type, pointed right at me and said, 'I see the sin-scarred faces of Blanket men, unsaved.' That just cost him five bucks I was going to throw in for expenses. And one gets the hip-sweeney standing while they sing and call for mourners. All in all, I do not think much of revivals. The church is a place for sanctity and dignity, or should be. The Creator did a wonderful thing when he made one day to be good in. It freshens one up. Then you can fall back for six more days. However, I do love the organ music and the singing, and if I still had my voice I would go oftener, the year around. The old hymns are fine and beautiful; you can have these so-called gospel singers that everyone listens to on the radio. I like it at the Church of Christ, they are very fine singers—they don't even need an organ. I like to hear the voices picking up as the leader starts forth:

'There is a habitation built by the living God

'For all of every nation who seek that grand abode . . .'

and then the chorus

Congregation at Mt. Adam

Skinning Deer

'Oh Zion, Zion, I long thy gates to see . . .'
and the bass singers, most of them big and bald and bass singers from Giles rumbling in with:

'Oh Zion, lovely Zion . . .'
Boy howdy, I could damn near see it."

Chapter 31

KELLY'S attitude toward his painting was at first one of only temporary preoccupation. It was as if he had found a weed in his pasture that not only had an interesting bloom but that could also be harvested and sold. He would do this only until he could get back on his feet (a conditional clause of fifty years of intimacy). Then he would devote his full attention to farming and horses once more.

He had sold his first water colors in 1946. Four years later, having in the meantime switched to oils, he had his one-man show at the Dallas Museum of Fine Arts. From that time on there was a steady demand for his work, and Kelly's feeling about his paintings became more positive and proprietary. He was pleased and flattered that people liked his work. He was amazed that, after a long life of failure and disappointment in a variety of endeavors, success was now coming to him in a field that he considered nothing more than a personal form of amusement. Now he lavished more and more loving care on his intricate compositions and the microscopically drawn figures.

He seldom sold a painting without becoming a friend of the buyer, nor did he ever sell to anyone he would not like to claim as a friend. In most cases a sale was followed by a steady correspondence with the owner. Kelly wrote letters with as much zest as he spoke; he drew little pictures on the margins and headings of his letters to illustrate his statements, his sentiments or the season—schooners of beer, horses of forthright maleness, Mexican *pastores*, German bartenders, onions and radishes springing from the ground, a blazing fireplace, children playing together. He would spend days drawing and illustrating a greeting card for a special friend, days that he might well have spent on serious painting.

Kelly paintings went to New York and California and the states in between, and there was a ready market for more. But as the demand rose his production retarded. With a little money coming in he had more time for riding his horse, making excursions to the hill country, reading, writing letters and visiting with the people who came to see him.

The Ford Motor Company commissioned him to do a series of paintings of Texas brush country to illustrate an article by J. Frank Dobie. The paintings appeared in the Lincoln-Mercury *Times*, and the Ford Company later presented the originals to Texas A&M, an institution which Kelly greatly admired, having once helped deliver a truckload of horses there. Kelly attended the presentation, smuggling in with him a flask of brandy swathed in a white handkerchief to fortify his courage. He was impressed with the chancellor of the school and the various knowing people who exclaimed over the quality of his work, but he was more impressed with Owen Garrigan, who was in charge of the horse barns.

Later the Ford Company commissioned him to both write and illustrate an article on his beloved hill country of Texas, but the assignment was never completed. He would finish one picture of the series only to have someone admire it so extravagantly that he could not refuse to sell it—and the money was always handy.

Two of his paintings were included in a collection of American paintings which the Smithsonian Institution sent on a European tour. Kelly was pleased, not so much by the honor as the fact that his paintings would be shown in Switzerland where his paternal grandfather had come from.

Francis Henry Taylor, then director of the Metropolitan Museum of New York, met Kelly during a visit to Texas, admired his paintings and bought one of them. Later he was to declare that Kelly was "one of the few genuine primitive painters we have had in our country," but Kelly was less impressed with the great man's discernment than he was with the jokes that Taylor liked to tell.

Various well-intentioned persons suggested slight alterations in Kelly's way of working—the most frequent suggestion being that he paint on larger canvases—with almost no effect. He would thank them kindly for their interest and go on working in his own way. Because he was fascinated with figure drawing, and learning much about it through trial and error, be began, slowly, to make his people and animals somewhat larger and bolder, but the change was almost imperceptible to any eye but Kelly's. He switched from canvas-textured paperboard to canvas-covered masonite and finally to gesso boards. Painting on gesso was more difficult and far slower (and he was a slow painter at best), but he conceded that the owners of his paintings deserved whatever guarantee of permanence he could give them.

His compositions always ran clear to the edge of the canvas as though the viewer were looking through a window, the window frame arbitrarily setting a boundary to the scene. Framed, with the rabbet covering a narrow border, the pictures frequently lost part of a person or animal. Kelly was disinclined to correct this. When Mrs. Stanley Marcus complained good-naturedly that framing had robbed her of several goats in one of her favorite Kelly paintings, Kelly promised that on his next trip to the Marcus home he would bring his paints and add a few goats in plain view: "We got plenty pasture there."

On rare occasions he would paint a picture to order, but in his own way. When Dallas lawyer Rudolph Johnson, a collector whom Kelly liked and admired, asked, tentatively, if Kelly would paint a picture of an oil rig with which he was hopefully drilling a wildcat well, Kelly agreed. He visited the well site, studied it and, in time, produced a painting that was completely Kelly and completely pastoral: a rocky hillside, grazing goats, a man on horseback. The oil rig was there but it was as natural and unobtrusive a part of the landscape as the mesquite trees.

He balked, however, at frequent requests from wealthy Texans to paint ranch scenes with Hereford cattle. The Herefords were a noble breed, he would concede, but a herd of Herefords had become a status symbol for lately arrived cattlemen, who, for the most part, Kelly could not abide.

"I am tired of pictures of Hereford bulls and cows that look like bathing beauties. I would like to see some old onion-eyed longhorns. I lost a sale last week to a rancher's wife because I said I was weary of looking at overstuffed Hereford bulls and heifers and preferred to paint Brahmans and mossy old longhorns and Mexican stock. To hell with them. They are so damn smug with rich oil relatives backing them and buying up the whole country. There are so many purebred Hereford breeders around that they must perforce sell to one another to stay in business.

"A much nobler picture for me is a big old Brahman bull, standing in the shade and waiting for a cow to come to him, not wasting his flesh 'walking' her for a day or so. A grand idea, although it hasn't worked too well for me. Maybe I haven't found the right tree, but anyhow I'm bowlegged from standing and waiting."

After the success of his one-man show at the Dallas Museum of Fine Arts, Kelly was invited to come be an "artist in residence" at the museum during state fair time. The Dallas Museum is located on the state fairgrounds, and each year director Jerry Bywaters arranged special exhibitions to interest the millions of people who came to see the largest annual exposition of its kind in the country. Kelly was perfect for the occasion. He came with his tin suitcase, his cardboard box of paints and brushes (an admirer had given him a handsome, compartmented metal case for his tools but it was never used) and a partially finished painting. He would establish himself in the court of the museum, place the painting on a low work table and seat himself on a stool. He would, intermittently, do a little work on the unfinished canvas, but mostly he talked with whoever stopped to see what he was doing. Sometimes he would wander away from the table, go out for a hard-boiled egg and a bottle of beer, visit the fairground horse barns or stop in at the girlie show on the midway. Refreshed, he would return to his table for a few more dabs at the painting and more conversation. Kelly loved it, but he could, if the occasion indicated, be sharp. One unthinking visitor, in a lame attempt at jocularity, asked, "Isn't it rather late at night for an old character like you to be out?" Kelly cut his eyes at the man, stared coolly and asked, "Can you break a horse?" The joker flushed and left, and Kelly went on with a story about Arizona in '04.

Although the price of his paintings had increased almost tenfold in the few years he had been painting, Kelly was always broke and he painted more and more slowly. He had, finally, qualified for Social Security ("I don't like the idea of it—nobody owes me anything, but I will say it's handy and keeps my friends from worrying about me"), but the monthly checks were still not enough to carry him between paintings. He regularly went to the bank and borrowed money. This, for Kelly, was a normal way to live. There was no temptation to speed up his painting or put it on a factory basis. There was enough money to keep the storm cellar stocked with beer, to buy little presents for his wife and daughter and grandsons and to make an occasional excursion to the hill country. What else did a man need money for?

More and more of his time was spent writing to his constantly widening circle of friends. Often at the top of his stationery he would draw a little coat of arms consisting of a horse, a jackass and a schooner of beer, with a title: "Great seal of the House of Kelly (H. O.): Horse ardent; Jack rampant; Beer potent; on field Verdant."

And he would write:

"I have got so now when I write at night I can't go to sleep. I get all charmed up. Always thinking of something else I want to say.

"I have not worked well this winter. Too many sneezes, hacks and hisses. How in hell can a fellow paint with his nose dripping and his eyes squinted up like a pig looking up a bare 'simmon tree? I shouldn't complain about winter, since we have so little of it. I often think of the old-fashioned winters in the East and up in Michigan and Wyoming, but I don't miss them. They are fine for kids and Christmas cards, but I've long since made peace with snow. I've had my part of it. Many's the time I envied a cow with her rump backed into a straw stack whilst I had to ride on and drag her less fortunate sisters out of the drifts.

"But spring is here now; you can always tell in Texas because of the cold northers; eighty-five degrees yesterday and thirty-seven today. This is probably the turtle-dove storm; we have two more to come—the Easter flurry and the blackberry winter. We had good winter rains and the fields are as green as a pool table. The farmers have got their fingers out of their shirt collars and the stockmen are all hoped up. The country is white, now, with new kids and lambs. Some goats are already shorn. The bulls are talking to themselves again, the top horses are restless and the boar hogs are taking the fences apart. I would start strutting myself, but it's early yet. And this winter I read *Don Quixote* again and I remember what happened to old Rosinante with the Galician mares.

"It is time for our state flower, poke (at least it *should* be, anyhow), to show. There are already ladies coming out to ask about it. I am fixing to get into difficulties. I have promised to notify too many women about the poke rising, unless there is a holy miracle and poke greens pop up all over the place. All of Blanket must at one time have got their poke greens along this little creek.

"Sometimes I wonder if I might not make a little business out of a matrimonial club. There are fifty-two widows in Blanket. I could write and illuminate little posters for them: 'Able-bodied, wealthy widow lady—can get into bed under her own power. Own home—modern.' One of the widows got married last week. She was at church on Sunday, but unaccompanied, thus testifying to the other ladies of her vitality. It was the first Sunday her man had missed church in years.

"I keep painting away, but I get tired and bored. I would like to go somewhere and live in sin and idleness, mostly sin. The women that come around here are too old or too fat—or they come in pairs. Marriage is a rather confining business. A man like myself should have at least three women: one, say, to teach school or work at some other paying job; one to cook and run a little café on the side where people would come to drink and eat and talk; and one just to take care of loose ends around the place.

170

"When I was a young bachelor back in Arkansas there was never a time but when the notion struck me I'd turn the stock into the river pasture, call my dog, strap my Winchester onto the saddle and ride back up into the hills, a country of potent white whisky and tender-eyed ladies. I get notions, yet, but your ideas change. Right now I'd just like to go down around Cameron and Bryan where they're working that chocolate-colored land. Smell mule sweat and see the cultivator sweeps slipping through that good, rich soil. And hear Negroes sing and ride out in the Bermuda grass pastures and see the big Brahmans. And go on tour around the state of Texas and visit all the little towns with the lovely names, Dripping Springs, Loyal Valley, Cherry Springs, Dime Box, Stonewall, Rising Star and Comfort. Well, enough of this wishing. It's time for me to go back to hell and gone in the mountains again— up on Salt Mountain or Burns Mountain or Rattlesnake Knob. I go alone because no one else wants to do what I do—drive along the lovely, winding narrow roads with pauses on the hilltops to view the panorama. Those trips are medicine for the bitter taste that boils up sometimes when one wants to do something and can't. As Newt Holt used to say, I would do it if I was able, and of course I'm able but I just ain't got the money.

"On the other hand, the hens are laying well, we already have little chicks hatched, the small garden is pretty with green things coming up, and Jess fixes me wonderful things to eat. Old Babe, the mare, like wine, improves with age, and I, like Mr. Micawber, look for something to turn up.

"Here I sit with my radio, surrounded by brazen-voiced hillbilly singers and pistol-head, jackleg, hickory-whittled, over-the-border preachers squalling like fresh-cut tomcats to save my soul and keep me from hearing the lovely German and Czech band music that I like, and I keep thinking of the drinking quartet with which I used to sing, making the rounds of Irish and German saloons (also the establishment of one madame, a fine woman and a handsome one). After the tenor flatted out we disbanded for the night. My brain was fine, but the street wasn't wide enough. I'd been sprinkling green pepper sauce in my ale and porter and I got home feeling like I had a wonderful, red handlebar mustache, well aled and portered.

"Yesterday my eyes played out, so I played hookey again. I saddled up and rode over west to a pasture and sat around under a live oak with the rest of the stock. I watched the horses go down to the stock tank and bathe and come out on the banks and play, rearing and wheeling and kicking. I sat so quietly jackrabbits grazed all around me and birds sang over my head. Then the horses came back and stood about shading and taking siesta. When they finally started off to graze I mounted and rode toward home. On the way I saw a flock of goats standing around a large tank. They formed a perfect circle. They were beautiful. They had been shorn and their new hair shone like silver in the sun. It was like silver candles on a cake.

"I like goats. I like sheep, too, but goats have character and a sense of humor. There are goats on the place adjoining us, and Jess and I greatly enjoy watching them. I'm sure we enjoy them more than the owner does, because we do not have to care for them. When they go over the hill we are done with them.

"Sometimes I think of how my grandmother used to say, 'When it rains broth we have no spoon.' There are so many beautiful things around me, and I have so many wonderful things stored in my head I wonder where I will find room for more. Do you remember what old Don Quixote said after he saw the divining ape? 'He who reads much and travels far sees much and learns a great deal.' Good night, and *vaya con Dios.*"

Chapter 32

"OLD Doc Cobb used to say," Kelly recalled, "that a man just learns to live along about the time his body is played out. The womenfolks have learned this faster than us men; they know how to take care of themselves, and the time of the tottery old grandma is long gone, thank God. I aim to study women more and more and learn how they do it, because I want to live to be a very old man, and a spry one, not like an old grandpa horse that's barely able to go. My ears aren't lopped. They are still pricked forward and I can still trot along and nicker and call to the girls. Else I would be painting funerals and resurrections and other bilious scenes.

"I've just begun to live. And, you know, it's a hard thing to say, but of all the different places I have lived since I started out for myself there's none of them that I have any desire to return to. It's not because of the work, worry, drouths, debt and hell—there was plenty of all that, but I forget it and just remembered the happy things. And I'd rather think about pleasant things today and tomorrow than way back then.

"They wanted me to come up to the state fair again, and I really wanted to go. When I think of all the good people that stopped by last year whilst I was painting and said, 'Well, good-by, Mr. Kelly, we hope we see you again next year,' it makes me very sad to be missing them. But then, hell, you can't have everything. This new young doctor I've got treating me, a heart specialist, a fine young fellow (and is his receptionist nice!), when he took me off potato chips (and is there anything in the store that looks better than nice fresh potato chips?), I saw it was time to stop, look and listen.

"Did I tell you how old Lee Stewart died? He was eighty-two. He said, 'I've sure had fun today,' and just died. Wasn't that nice? He was a great old horseman, the only one I ever knew that neither drank nor smoked, and a wagon-train driver from the old days. He wasn't afraid of any damn thing. And somehow it made me think of where it says in Job: 'At destruction and famine thou shalt laugh: neither shalt thou be afraid of the beasts of the earth. For thou shalt be in league with the stones of the field: and the beasts of the field shall be at peace with thee. . . . Thou shalt come to thy grave in a full age, like as a shock of corn cometh in his season.' Now those are verses for a horseman, stockman or farmer.

"I wish I could apply myself more to my painting. I'm always playing hooky and hunting waltz and polka records and talking to people on the road to and fro when I should be painting. I expect to make a lot of pictures yet. Hell, I'm just getting well started." He had a supply of canvases with the unchanging blue skies already painted in, waiting for the hills and fields, sturdy houses, handsome animals and happy people.

Two weeks before his quick and easy death in the seventy-second year of his life Kelly was writing to an old friend. As he so often did, he was writing on whatever scraps of paper he happened to find in a cluttered drawer. He came, finally, to a sheet of blue paper, a light, cheerful blue that was almost exactly the color he used for his skies.

"Oh, here is a page the color the whole sky was the other morning, plumb to the earth," he wrote. "It was like looking through a blue window light. You just wouldn't believe it without seeing it, and you'll never see it unless you come back home to Texas. But, to be honest, I do not remember ever having seen a sky quite that blue myself. And I have always been quite observant of natural phenomena."

Acknowledgments

MANY people have helped make this book a reality. The author particularly wishes to express his appreciation to Jessie Kelly, Martha Kelly Eoff, Margaret McCutcheon, Philip M. Kelly, Tom Lea, Jerry and Mary Bywaters, Henderson Shuffler, Charles and Maurine Stewart, Dan and Mary Longwell, David Gordon Hay, Richard B. Bell, Newt Holt, Dewey Decker, Wesley Hudgins, Jim Gorman, Lawrence Ashby, Albert Law, W. H. Kittrell, Col. Lawrence Westbrook, Rudolph Johnson, Stanley and Billie Marcus, Fred C. Cutter, John L. Paxton, Ed Nabors, B. J. Stevens, the late E. De-Golyer, Everett L. DeGolyer, Jr., the late Francis Henry Taylor, Henry Allen Moe, James F. Mathias, Savoie Lottinville, Frank Wardlaw, J. Frank Dobie, Lee Barker, Charles Morton, Ned Bradford, Bennett Cerf, Hardwick Moseley, Edward K. Thompson, Joe Scherschel, James Shepley, Richard Clurman, Frank McCulloch, T. George Harris, Marylois Purdy, the Rev. E. J. Morgan, Jess Gressett, Doris Lee, Jill Kornblee, Arthur T. Lougee, many anonymous but helpful librarians in the public libraries of Los Angeles and Beverly Hills, to Claire Perry for her great help in preparing the manuscript, and most of all to my wife for her patience, enthusiasm, and encouragement.

William Weber Johnson

Encino
January 1960.